Muhammad

gabriel
mandel khân

Muhammad
the prophet

THUNDER BAY
P · R · E · S · S
San Diego, California

ART DIRECTOR
Giorgio Seppi

MANAGING EDITOR
Tatjana Pauli

DESIGN AND LAYOUTS
Elena Dal Maso

COVER
Federico Magi

MAPS
Margil, Milan

ENGLISH TRANSLATION
Jay Hyams

TYPESETTING
Michael Shaw

ALL THE PHOTOGRAPHS IN THIS BOOK ARE BY
Max Mandel

NOTE TO THE READER

The original edition of this book was printed exactly one month before the events of September 11, 2001. Certain aspects of this book, most of all its expressions of the frustrations and disappointments of Muslim peoples, can be seen to foreshadow those events; other aspects, most of all those that deal with the realities of the Islamic religion and its traditions, should offer English-speaking readers reassurance and hope for the future. The bibliography at the end of the book provides both old and new routes for further understanding these all-important issues.
—The Editors

 Thunder Bay Press
An imprint of the Advantage Publishers Group
THUNDER BAY 5880 Oberlin Drive, San Diego, CA 92121-4794
P · R · E · S · S www.thunderbaybooks.com

© 2001 Mondadori Electa S.p.A., Milan

English translation © 2004 Mondadori Electa S.p.A., Milan
All rights reserved.

ISBN 1-59223-401-1

Library of Congress Cataloging-in-Publication Data available upon request.

Printed and bound in Spain by Artes Gráficas Toledo, SA

1 2 3 4 5 09 08 07 06 05

Contents

Preface

The patriarch Abraham invited all peoples to worship one God, absolute and eternal. From him are descended the three revealed monotheistic religions: Judaism, Christianity, and Islam. The sacred text of Judaism, the Old Testament, or Hebrew Bible, was formulated over the course of ten centuries with contributions from a host of prophets, rabbis, and preachers. The sacred texts of Christianity—the four Gospels, Acts, the twenty-one Epistles, and Revelation—were compiled over the period of a century, principally by the apostles Peter and Paul.

The Koran "descended" upon a single man, Muhammad, over a period of about twenty-three years. Muhammad began the transmission of the Koran to the world, at first in the face of hostility, in a difficult land among a resistant and malevolent people. Inspired by God, moved by divine grace, he was the bearer of a sacred word that animated and still animates the religion that today claims the greatest number of followers in the world, a religion that the West is now reluctantly being forced to confront. The Koran contains the words of Islam with which Muhammad, an outstanding socioeconomic and political organizer as well as a religious leader, formed a barbarous, divided, and unknown people into a force that in a hundred years conquered much of the world, consolidating its various great cultures within a single, enormous synthesis. In the course of its first ten centuries, Islam gave the West great gifts in the fields of the medical sciences, mathematics, astronomy (including the concept of the roundness of the Earth and the existence of the Americas), as well as physics, chemistry, and agriculture; and transmitted to Europe, among other things, paper and printing, Arabic numerals, polychrome ceramics, irrigation, and the idea of universities.

Such makes clear the historical importance of Muhammad, the "Seal of the Prophecy," the earthly existence of whom is traced in this book by way of an investigation that is as historical, objective, exhaustive, and impartial as possible.

Arabia Before Muhammad

*It was the time of the ancient ignorance (Koran 33:33).
Their gods induced many to make idols and to slay their
children that they might ruin them and throw the
cloak of confusion over their religion (6:137).
They committed turpitudes (6:151) and buried
their female children alive (81:8).*

ARABIA FELIX, HINGE OF THREE CONTINENTS

The Arabian Peninsula, the largest peninsula in the world, is a quadrilateral about 1,200 miles long and roughly 1,300 miles wide at its widest point. To the east it is bordered by the Persian Gulf, to the south by the Arabian Sea and the Gulf of Aden, to the west by the Red Sea, and to the north by an imaginary line running from the mouth of the Tigris River to the Gulf of Aqaba. Its inhabitants know it as Jazirat al Arab, "the Island of the Arabs," a strange name since the peninsula is firmly attached to Asia, but just as every island separates its inhabitants from a continent, slowing or preventing contact with the mainland and creating a kind of psychological

separation—along with a sclerotic traditionalism—so it has been and still is today with Arabia.

The world's most important settled civilizations arose along river valleys: there are no such valleys on the Arabian Peninsula. Elsewhere in the world, central mountain ranges prevent excessive temperature ranges: here, there are no such mountains. For many countries, the sea has favored cultural exchanges along with daring voyages far from the national borders, but the coast of Arabia is poor in ports and islands, and the Arabs are not navigators. The result is that the primary division between Arabia and the rest of the world is a matter of culture. On one side is the Fertile Crescent, cradle of many civilizations, open to change, intrigued by foreign cultures and capable of understanding them, a land across which peoples and ideas flow freely; on the other is a peninsula inhabited by relatively homogeneous populations lacking in new ideas and resistant both to culture and to change.

The very shape of the Arabian Peninsula is a cause of this. Flying over it, one is struck by the great variety of this vast desert, spotted with the rare oasis in its interior and bordered by a few inhabited areas along its coasts. The high peaks in the extreme south are followed by a series of hills, punctuated with the geometric masses of plateaus, then lower hills crossed by broad bands of sand like brightly colored abstract paintings. These various rocky landscapes form a ring around a central zone, half of which is covered by a vast, sandy desert, the Rub al-Khali, the "Empty Quarter," followed to the north by the arid plateaus of Nadid, Nafud, and the Dahna.

Vegetation must contend not only with the aridity of the environment but with the salinity of the soil. Few plants can grow in these conditions. There are low, spiny bushes, and the occasional acacia, but most of all there is the date palm, the fruit of which often constitutes the only food for humans and camels alike. No fewer than one hundred varieties of this plant are known. There are times when the air in the center of the peninsula is so dry that it is almost without oxygen; moving toward the coast, the presence of water increases. The areas where it is found burst with life, and the valleys cut by torrents are blessed with lush vegetation. Violent rains can suddenly pour down after two or three years of steady drought. Only in Yemen and Asir are the periodic squalls sufficient to permit regular cultivation, resulting in perennial vegetation, rich and lush, with a strong fragrance. Sanaa, the capital of Yemen, is 7,250 feet above sea level and is the largest and most salubrious city of Arabia. Hadhramawt and Oman, to the extreme south, are also rainy and verdant. Of all the peninsula, those zones—known as the Green Crescent—are the best for human settlement. Incense trees flower there, and in the Asir acacias are found. Coffee, the boast of the Red Sea, was brought to southern Arabia from Ethiopia in the fourteenth century (according to the

seventeenth-century Italian traveler Pietro della Valle, it was unknown in Europe until 1650; other sources indicate 1589). The tamarisk, pomegranate, apple, apricot, almond, orange, lemon, watermelon, sugarcane, and banana originated in the south and spread to other areas of the peninsula.

The most common animals are panthers, leopards, hyenas, wolves, foxes, and lizards. There are also horses, donkeys, dogs (most notably greyhounds), cats, sheep, and goats. Once there were lions, but they have disappeared; a few monkeys still hold on in Yemen and Saudi Arabia. But just as the date palm is the queen of plants, the king of animals is the camel, a means of transport domesticated since the first

Opposite top: Eighth-century ceramic in the shape of a Bedouin couple on a camel.

Opposite bottom: Wild camels at Jebel Yatib, Saudi Arabia.

Top: Bedouin tent at Darb Zubaida.

Left: Arabian camel in a relief at the Apadana Palace of Darius at Persepolis, Iran.

millennium BC. The camel is the Arabian animal par excellence, the companion of man and his indispensable support in a region truly hostile to survival. Without the camel, the pre-Islamic south Arabian civilizations would never have come into being.

Placed like a hinge at the juncture of three continents, the Arabian Peninsula has a little of Europe, Africa, and Asia. To the ancient Romans it was Arabia Felix: "Fortunate Arabia." A vast container of peoples, it was once believed to have been the cradle of the Semites, a people thought to have departed the peninsula to found the nearby countries of the Akkadians, the Chaldeans, the Aramaeans, the Canaanites, and today's Arabs. These are peoples that—perhaps as a result of vicinity, cultural affinity, and historical-political events— spoke similar languages leading back to a single original language. The term *Semite* comes from the Bible (Genesis 9:18: "And the sons of Noah, that went forth of the ark, were Shem [Sem], and Ham, and Japeth."), but truly no such "Semitic race" has ever existed, nor any ethnic unity among the above-mentioned peoples.

Above: Map of Ibn Khurradadhbih, ca. 846.

Below: Cave tomb at Wadi Dab, Yemen.

Opposite top: House in San'a, Yemen.

Opposite bottom: Tamith, a pre-Islamic south Arabian idol.

Palaces as Tall as Skyscrapers

The geographic position of the Arabian Peninsula, the nature of its terrain, the conditions of its settled peoples and its nomads, and most of all the qualities in the regions of southern Arabia that produced spices and incense all contributed to one of the most important trade routes of the ancient world, the Great Caravan Route, or the Incense Road. It was similar to the Silk Route along which the products of the Far East were brought from China to the Mediterranean. Along this route, which led from oasis to oasis across deserts, goods were carried on the backs of camels. Thus, such luxury products as spices for foods, refined Indian fabrics, and the incense necessary for sacred rites and embalming were brought to the Egyptians and to the Mesopotamians and then later to the Greeks, Romans, and Byzantines.

The route began at the ports of the southern coast (Salala, Sailhun, Bhir, Mukalla, Aden), where products arrived from India (thus the Greeks believed they came from southern Arabia). These goods, along with local products, especially incense, were stored in the cities of the small south Arabian kingdoms, such as Shabwa, Zafar, Marib, and Ma'in. They were then taken north by way of Mecca, moving parallel to the coast but avoiding the banks of the Red Sea and moving instead across the plateau, skirting the mountains to reach Petra and the Mediterranean port of Gaza. There were four main pre-Islamic southern Arabian kingdoms, each named for its people: the Saba (Sheba), Ma'in (Minaean), Qataban, and Hadhramawt.

Saba was perhaps the most important of these kingdoms; it is the best known, both for the visit of the queen of Sheba to Solomon (mentioned in the Bible and the Koran) and for an impressive construction, the great dam near its capital, Marib, 1,000 feet long, fifty feet high, and 120 feet wide at the base. Minaean inscriptions found on the Greek island of Delos and at Al Fayyum in Egypt indicate that the kingdom's trading centers were widely distributed. The Qataban capital was Tumn'a, in its time an important caravan center. The commercial and religious center of Hadhramawt was Shabwa, grand enough to be mentioned by both Eratosthenes and Pliny.

The capitals of these south Arabian kingdoms were famous for their large palaces, such as the castle of Ghumdan

Who Are the Arabs?

Who are the Arabs of the Arabian Peninsula, and where did they come from? Even today the answer remains a mystery, and none of the many theories put forward seems completely acceptable, primarily because of the lack of systematic paleoanthropological studies. They were originally nomadic populations, and such populations are known to travel over thousands of miles. The Huns, for example, after attacking China (part of the Great Wall was built to keep them out), turned around, invaded Europe, and formed the empire of Attila, whose invasion resulted in refugees founding Venice, Italy.

In all probability the oldest Arab nucleus was composed of mountain dwellers of Yemen; without doubt, these people were crosses of Mediterranean peoples (Bedouins of the north) with others, including Veddoid peoples (the tribes of Mahra and others). The Arabs themselves recognize a duality of origin: there are the "original" or "true Arabs" of the south, descendants of Qahtan (identified as the biblical Joktan) and the "Arabized Arabs" of the north, descendants of Adnan (great-grandchild of Ishmael). But according to other versions, the only authentic Arabs are the "Vanished" (or "Disappeared") Arabs of whom the Koran speaks. The first historical indication of Arabs are references to Aramaic Bedouins who, in 880 BC, intervened in the questions of the Beit Zamani, in the upper Euphrates. In 854 BC an Arabian king named Gindibu led a thousand camel riders from Arabia to Karkar (Qarqar) to help Bir Idri of Damascus (the Benhadad of the Bible) battle Shalmaneser III. Information about Arabs begins to increase in Assyria during the reigns of Tiglathpileser, 745–726 BC, and Sargon II, 722–705 BC; there is also mention of great priestly queens, of peripheral kingdoms that refused to pay tribute, and of central kingdoms that ruled collections of oases and already traded in incense and camels.

A clarification is needed. It is true that from earliest times, successive waves of Arabs have pushed outward into the surrounding areas, and that with Islam they reached as far as central Asia, but these were always limited groups destined to be either driven out or absorbed into the local populations without leaving a trace. Therefore, only the inhabitants of the Arabian Peninsula are considered specifically "Arabs," while the populations of North Africa and the Fertile Crescent (from the Sinai to Iraq) are Arabic-speaking but not Arabic. Of course, from the very earliest European studies, all Muslims in Mediterranean countries have been looked upon in general as Arabs, in large part because of the apparent homogeneity attributed to these peoples during the Islamic period by the Koran, according to which all of them spoke dialects derived from Arabic.

The error has become so deeply rooted that even today Arabic-speaking peoples are referred to as Arabs if only for simplicity of understanding. There are, however, differences. The Palestinians, for example, were an Illyrian population; from Albania they traveled by sea to the coast of Egypt. Unable to conquer Egypt, they withdrew to the "Lands of the Middle," a sort of no-man's-land. That they were Sea Peoples (Pelagians) shows up in their name itself: Pelagasians, Philistines, Palestinians.

The Moroccans resulted from a union of the Vandals (hence Vandalusia, which became Andalusia) with the Maures of the Grand Atlas Mountains.

Opposite top: The temple of Marib at San'a, Yemen.

Top: Head of an ancestor, pre-Islamic south Arabian art.

Left: Pre-Islamic south Arabian inscription.

at Azal (contemporary Sanaa, in Yemen). It was built around 25 BC, and according to the historians of its time it had twenty floors, the first in stone, the last in polished marble. It was crowned by four carved lions and a terrace with a ceiling of transparent alabaster. Damaged by the Abyssinians in 525 and rebuilt by the Persians in 570, it was demolished by the Muslim conqueror Farwa ibn Musayk.

According to the Greek geographer and historian Strabo (64 BC–AD 24), the south Arabian caravans covered the distance from Marib to Aqaba in seventy days. As the Mediterranean peoples gradually became more prosperous, refined, and also decadent, the demand for the products of south Arabia increased to the point that the Yemeni merchants were among the world's richest; today's oil has replaced yesterday's incense.

This immense wealth attracted the greedy eyes of many people, but the merchants involved in the trade were well protected by the desert around them, and until the collapse of the south Arabian commercial kingdoms, they could also count on their own forces. To get around them, efforts were made to locate another route. The Egyptian king Ptolemy II (reigned 285–246 BC) reopened the Nile–Red Sea canal that had been dug by

Sesostris seventeen centuries earlier. In the second century BC, the Greek navigator Eudoxus of Cyzicus explored routes across the Red Sea, exploiting monsoons and currents, and the navigator Hippalus established the Indian Ocean route that allowed Romans to reach India and open trade centers there. In 60 BC, Petra became a vassal of Rome, and in 24 BC it helped the Roman general Aelius Gallus in an expedition to conquer Yemen, an expedition that ended in disastrous defeat. The Roman emperor Trajan dealt a decisive blow to south Arabian commerce in AD 105 by annexing Petra to the Roman

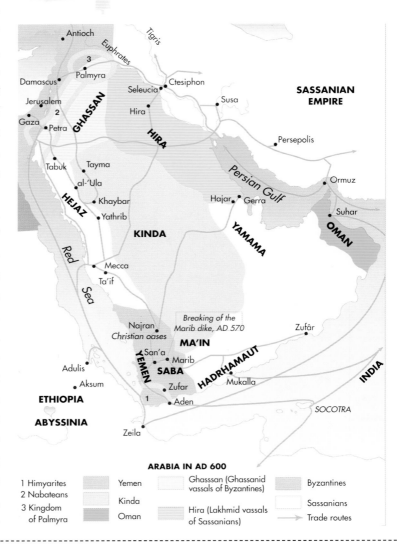

ARABIA IN AD 600

1 Himyarites	Yemen	Ghassan (Ghassanid vassals of Byzantines)	Byzantines
2 Nabateans	Kinda		Sassanians
3 Kingdom of Palmyra	Oman	Hira (Lakhmid vassals of Sassanians)	Trade routes

CENTRAL ARABIA, HOMELAND OF MUHAMMAD

The time was the seventh century AD. The place was central Arabia, a region populated by nomadic tribes, with a few caravan towns and large oases. The inhabitants lived in groups based on the unit of the clan, which served their common defense and was bolstered by the code of blood revenge (*thar*). The clans were joined in tribes locked in ceaseless hostility with other tribes; at any time any one of the tribes could exercise its right to raid and plunder another.

At the same time, the Yemeni kingdoms were getting rich with gold and also with works of Mediterranean art imported for their monetary value, and while classical historians wrote effusively about southern Arabia, the Bedouins of the desert knew nothing of stability, civilization, or written history. On the other hand, they were free, proud, and tightly bound by unwritten laws. Every tent represented a family, every camp a clan; a collection of clans formed a tribe. Because of the hostility of the environment, the members of each tribe were bound by ties far stronger than those of nationalism; the tribe was the enemy of all other peoples, the only exceptions being loose, temporary associations formed out of shared interests. The outlaw who deserted his tribe set himself against everyone and could no longer depend on help

Opposite: Pre-Islamic Arabia around AD 600.

Bottom: Camel and driver at Jebel Saidi.

Above: Hydraulic complex of the kingdom of Saba, Yemen.

Empire. Deprived of their northern outlet, the south Arabians began to support Persia (first the Parthians, then the Sassanids), perhaps not realizing that these powers tended to draw traffic in their direction, away from the Persian Gulf to routes along the Euphrates and all the way to Palmyra. The decline of the great Mediterranean empires and the drop in the large-scale importation of goods; the increasing political separation among Asia, Africa, and Europe; the progressive drying of southern Arabia; and the opening of new trade routes all led to the decline of the south Arabian kingdoms, which fell to battling among themselves in small local wars. Signs of the effects of the zone's progressive drying up are still visible today, but it is clear that the decline of the classical world took with it southern Arabia. This occurred without completely eliminating the Great Caravan Route, which was still active during the time of Muhammad.

each headed by a family leader who had full powers. When he thought it best to diminish the size of the clan to ensure its survival in times of famine, he ordered the wives to eliminate useless mouths, meaning to bury alive the youngest daughters.

from his clan, represented by its oldest or wisest member, the sheikh (from *shaykh*, Arabic for "elder"). The Bedouin obeyed only himself, and this fierce individuality probably explains the acceptance of the life imposed by the desert, a life of privations and fatigue.

For the nomads as well as for the settled peoples of central Arabia, tribal spirit united those who declared themselves descendants of the same leader or who obeyed an elected clan leader: the *sayyid*. Every tribe was composed of a group of families,

The Koran recalls this: *When the birth of a daughter is announced to any one of them, dark shadows settle on his face, and he is sad. He hideth him from the people because of the ill tidings: shall he keep it with disgrace or bury it in the sand?* (16:58–59). *Kill not your children for fear of want: for them and for you will we provide. Verily, the killing them is a great*

Above: Pre-Islamic ritual stone circle, Yemen.

Below: Archaeological site of Qurayya, Saudi Arabia.

Opposite top: Archaeological site of al-Khuraina, Saudi Arabia.

Opposite bottom: Rock graffiti at Jebel Yatib, Saudi Arabia.

Not all tribes followed the same customs and had such scant regard for women; in some cities there were female poets and merchants, as well as women who practiced medicine.

The clan protected the individual and responded to his actions according to age-old customs, traditions, and habits, thus also ruling out any evolution in the society or in the individual.

The tribe's defense of its goods and the honor of its individual members resulted in blood feuds, and among these nomads the raid had evolved into an ordinary part of life, aspects that might make the tribes of ancient Arabia seem like little more than organized brigands. At the same time, they had a strong spirit of hospitality and were always ready to help neighbors. Among the traits they most admired were eloquence, generosity, courage, and virility. As was then true nearly everywhere in the world, slavery was an accepted institution among the peoples of the Arabian Peninsula. Most slaves were black Africans, but they faced no particular prejudice and, when freed, mixed their blood with that of the tribe. Black people were living in the villages of al-Alfaj, in the heart of Arabia, and in no area of Arabia—as would later be true of the Islamic religion—was there discrimination on the basis of skin color.

wickedness! (17:31). *Slay not your children because of poverty: for them and for you we will provide* (6:151).

Polygamy, temporary marriages, and temporary exchanges of wives were common. To repudiate one's wife was easy, facilitated by the fact that the husband was under no obligation to make compensation to the repudiated wife. The wife could also divorce her husband. All she needed to do was present herself to him naked in public, or, during his absence change the orientation of their tent. Even so, women could not inherit and were themselves inherited by the firstborn son of the head of the family; they were ranked as chattel, at the same level as the rest of the inherited personal property.

The Major Cities of Arabia in the Seventh Century

Life was different in the cities along the caravan route and in the settled areas that had arisen around the major oases. These were cosmopolitan, with mixed populations. The trade had attracted agents and representatives from other lands, most of all Jews. In Hejaz, the opulent oasis of Khaybar was in the hands of Israelites, and Hebrew families were to be found throughout the region. At Yathrib (later Medina) the Jews lived in clans, closed within fortified homes, and held monopolies on various artisan crafts. They loaned money with interest (usury) and organized commerce. So it was along the length of the peninsula, all the way to Yemen, where the gold trade was in their hands. The Hebrew religion was the dominant faith in that

region, most of all early in the sixth century.

The most important city, and perhaps also the largest, was Mecca (or Makka, and called Macoraba by Ptolemy), which was in the hands of the Quraysh (from *qirsh*, meaning "shark," which was their emblem). In the fifth century, Qusayy, son of Kilab,

had led the Quraysh in wresting control of the city from the hands of the Khuza'a. The Quraysh had organized themselves in terms of both commerce (they were located at the center of the Great Caravan Route for incense) and religion. An idol of every divinity from the surrounding region existed at Mecca, but the "idol" embraced by all the religions was the Ka'ba, a small, nearly cubic construction that stood in the center of the city. According to tradition, it had been built by Abraham with the help of his son Ishmael, founder of the Arabs. The southeast corner of the Ka'ba enclosed the Black Stone, a dark piece of porphyry, today worn hollow by the kisses of the faithful. All around the Ka'ba stood the various quarters inhabited by the Quraysh clans, surrounded in turn by the areas inhabited by groups of foreign merchants, Jews, Christians, and Bedouins.

Each year the Arabic tribes of the region made two pilgrimages to Mecca: a small pilgrimage (*umra*) during the seventh month of the lunar year, and a large pilgrimage (*hajj*) during the eleventh, twelfth, and first months of the lunar year. These months were periods of "holy peace," and animals sent for sacrifice to Mecca were adorned with garlands so they would not be stolen along the road. As guardians of the sanctuary, the Quraysh enjoyed a similar kind of immunity, and their caravans, considered sacred, were not attacked by Bedouins.

The Quraysh reaped commercial rewards from the pilgrims, but to further profit from the situation, they distributed pilgrimage-related activities to their clans. The clan of the Hashimites (of which Muhammad was to be part) had the privilege of distributing water to the pilgrims from the Zamzam, the fountain

Opposite top: Remains of the great house at the oasis of Khaybar, Saudi Arabia. Opposite bottom: Lihyanite cave tomb, Yemen. Right: Recto and verso of a paleo-Islamic propitiatory tablet, Saudi Arabia.

Left: View of Mount Hira, overlooking Mecca.
Above: Sassanian coins.
Below: Arsacid coins.

Opposite top: Adam and Eve; Turkish miniature from the seventeenth century, Topkapi Palace Library, Istanbul.
Opposite bottom: Arrival of the Magi; fresco from Agac Alti Kilise, fifth century, Turkey.

that flowed beside the Ka'ba; the Umayyad (a clan that was to give two future caliphs, Uthman and Muawiya, the first Umayyad caliph) were the special standard bearers; the Nawfal collected offerings and distributed food to the pilgrims; the burgomaster was chosen from among the Asad; the Makhzum (one of whom would be the great Muslim general Khalid, son of Walid) saw to the weapons and commanded the cavalry. The Taym Khattab resolved questions of honor; the Adi (from whom would come the caliph Umar) oversaw friendly relations among the vendors; the Jumahiti were in charge of the oracles; the Sahm arbitrated conflicts and collected offerings. The Makhzum and the Umayya were the two richest clans. Arrogant and avaricious, they owned splendid country villas in the oasis of Taif, famous for its gardens and summer coolness.

All these privileges and the warehouses located in the areas of greatest interest on the peninsula (which by association enjoyed the privilege of being sacred) represented sources of great income. It is not difficult to understand why the Quraysh were violently hostile to the absolute monotheism preached by Muhammad.

THE RELIGIOUS AND POLITICAL SITUATION

In general, the pagan Arabs did not believe in an afterlife. They worshipped divinities, performed sacrifices, and undertook pilgrimages to Mecca in the hope of earthly well-being, but with no thought for the future. Their worship was thus much like magic, and magicians, wizards, fortune-tellers, and, most of all, poets were of great importance. The poet (*sha'ir*) was considered to be a blessing to his tribe. He inveighed against the enemy before raids and battles, and was a prophet, an invoker of curses, a verbal avenger, and also the narrator of the tribe's deeds, its historian, its exalter. Annual gatherings of poets took place in important centers like Sanaa, capital of Yemen, and

Ukad, Sihar, Maina, Duuamat, and al-Jandal. The winning poems were inscribed in gold letters on fabric and hung from the walls of the Ka'ba (the *mu'allaqat:* the "suspended," or "hung").

Greco-Roman mythology survived in Yemen, dominated by the local trinity: the Moon (a positive, male divinity), the Sun (a negative, female divinity), and Venus (their daughter). Each tribe had its own divinity, daughter of the most important god, expressed in the feminine in keeping with the Arabian custom that sees everything dangerous and baleful as feminine in order to lessen its power.

Some of these divinities were bizarre: the Hudhayl had Suwa, symbolizing sudden ejaculation; the Madhhidj worshipped Yaghuth (whose name means "he brings mercy"); the Banu

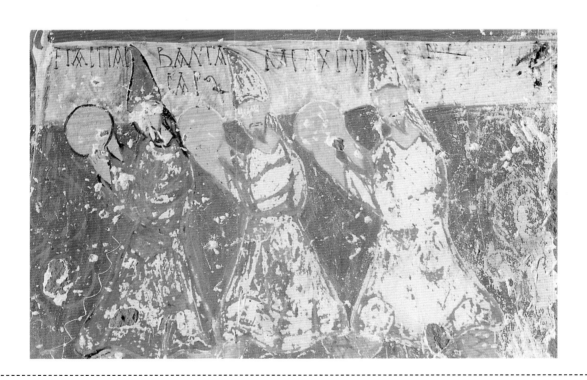

Kalbla worshipped Wadd (meaning "tender affection"), represented by an armed man; the Kula tribe had their god Nesr (a vulture); the Hamdan idolized Yaghuth (or Yahuk: "he prevents"). The last three divinities are mentioned in the Koran (71:23). Arab paganism was declining, but it was a slow decay and a supreme god was slowly taking shape among all the pagan divinities: al-Lah, a sort of Adonai, a god with an ineffable name.

Trade had an impact on the state of religion. Trade meant that Mecca—much like Yemen—was visited by merchants from every country of the ancient world, and many others set up permanent residence there, bringing along idols and other symbols of their gods. There were thus many divinities and much exchanging of ideas, with long, lively discussions at the way stations of the caravan route as well as in the cities awaiting the caravans' arrival. Of particular importance was the presence of Jews, great traders par excellence, for they brought their highly codified religion, their

Above: Column with pre-Islamic divinities, Nemrut Dag, Turkey.
Below: The Deir of Petra, Jordan, with the pre-Islamic sacred space.

Opposite top: Map with Mecca (above) and Medina (below).
Opposite bottom: Pre-Islamic stele depicting the divinity al-Ula, or Taima, Saudi Arabia.

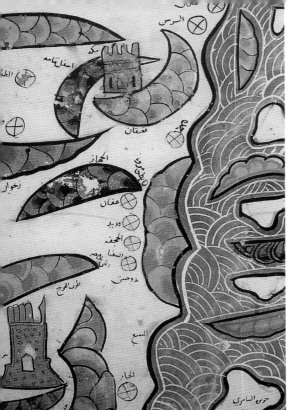

especially respected, they were not followed.

This situation of extreme religious fluidity was matched by political realities. Early in the seventh century, the pagan Persian empire of the Sassanids had extended its rule into Mesopotamia and given its protection to the Lakhmid state of Hira, also pagan, making it a buffer zone between Mesopotamia and the Arab tribes. The Orthodox

zealous religiosity and analytical character, and most of all their various holy books. The Jewish religion thus proliferated, along with various Christian sects (Byzantine Orthodox, Syrian and Ghassanid Monophysitism, Nestorianism, Catholicism, Arianism, as well as Abyssinian and Egyptian Copts and finally Gnosticism); on the pagan side there were the Iraqi and Sassanid Gnosticism and the various eponymous and tribal divinities.

Turning away from the materialism of the powerful Meccan clans, the pluralism of the pagan divinities, and the changeable nature of the Christian and Jewish sectarianism, some men of Mecca—true pioneers of the Sufi mysticism of Islam (the philosopher Poltinus was an example in Rome)—preferred the intimate search for a sense of a purely monotheistic divinity, free from all formality and ritual. These men came to be called *hunafa* (singular *hanif*), and while they were

Christian Byzantines ruled Jordan and Syria along with a good part of North Africa and supported their own buffer state, that of the Ghassanids, on the border between Syria and Arabia. The Abyssinians, being Christian Copts, sided with the Byzantines, as did the Christian Arabs, while the polytheists sided with the Persians.

The fate of Najran, a region and capital city in northern Yemen, is emblematic of this fluidity of peoples, religions, and power. Located at a crossroads of many caravan routes, it was the site of a colony of Jewish traders. So thoroughly did these traders control the local competition that some Himyarite tribes in the area converted to Judaism, while others converted to Christianity, which was being espoused by a young Arab of a noble family: Abdulla, son of Thamir. Then, however, Monophysite Christians began arriving in Najran, fleeing the religious persecution of the Byzantine emperor Justin I in northern Arabia. The Jewish monopoly declined to the point that the Jews went to war against the Christian trading companies and all the Christians in the area. The war ended in a massacre at Ukhdud, in which the Christians were hacked to death or burned alive by the hundreds.

The event caused a great sensation among the Byzantine Orthodoxy, in Coptic Abyssinia, and to a lesser degree in pagan Persia. The Abyssinian negus Alla Ashiha (Ella Asbeha) retaliated by going to war against the Himyarite king Dhu Nuwas, a Jew, and defeated and exiled him around 525. He then returned to Abyssinia, leaving a Coptic garrison at Dhafur. Dhu Nuwas reorganized his forces, attacked the garrison at Dhafur, and forced all the Christians in the city to take refuge in the church, which was then set on fire. He then called on all the Jews and pagans in his kingdom to massacre the Christians without exception. He slowly reconquered all of the country and in the end, thanks to the help of his general Dhu Yazan—who became a popular hero in Yemeni legends—he besieged Najran, where all the surviving Christians had taken refuge. He destroyed the churches, broke up the crosses, burned the Bibles, and ordered the Christians to convert to Judaism (the situation was thus extremely anomalous, since Jews rarely accept converts and consider as Jews only those born of a

Opposite top: Zoroastrian temple of fire worshippers at Surakhany, Azerbaijan.

Opposite bottom: Pre-Islamic Ghassanid ceramic, Islamic Institute of Oriental Archaeology, Amman.

Left: Scene of royal adoration, Mesopotamian relief. The image atop the altar may be an idealization of the Ka'ba.

Bottom: Plaque with cross on historical site of Najran, southern Arabia.

Jewish mother). By then Adbulla was a bishop, and under his leadership the Christians refused to convert. They were forced to dig a large trench that was then filled with wood and made into a pyre, onto which the Jewish king—according to chronicles of the times—had more than twenty thousand Christians thrown, including Saint Arethas. This was in 523. Dhu Nuwas asked Munzin, king of Hira, and Khosru of Persia to do the same in their territories. The Koran (85:1-9) refers to this massacre: *By the star-spangled heaven! By the promised day! By the witness and the witnessed! Cursed the masters of the trench, of the fuel-fed fire, when they sat around it, witnesses of what they inflicted on the believers! Nor did they torment them but for their faith in God, the Mighty, the Praiseworthy: His kingdom is of the heavens and of the earth; and God is the witness of everything. Verily, those who vexed the believers, men and women, and repented not, doth the torment of Hell and the torment of the burning await.*

Honoré de Balzac

"The life of Mahomet—a figure in whom the magic of Sabaeanism combined with the oriental poetry of the Hebrew Scriptures to result in one of the greatest human epics, the Arab dominion."
Honoré de Balzac (1799-1850),
Gambara

The Life of the Prophet

Did he not find thee an orphan and give thee a home?
And found thee erring and guided thee, and found thee
needy and enriched thee? (Koran 93:6-8)
O Prophet, Allah and such of the faithful as follow thee,
will be all-sufficient for thee (8:64).

زمدینه یهودیلرینه خبر اولدی انلردخی باشقه برجماعت

جمعه اولادی ایاه انله دخ طشه کادید اموز زقطون

WHEN MUHAMMAD WAS BORN

After the massacre at Najran, the Byzantine emperor called on the negus to intervene. In May of 525, an Ethiopian armada of about sixty to seventy thousand men under the command of generals Aryat and Abraha al-Ashram landed in Yemen. Dhu Nuwas, abandoned by the pagan tribes, was defeated; his general Dhu Yazan committed suicide by riding his horse into the Red Sea.

The Ethiopian Abraha, finding himself governor of the region, began in turn to raid and massacre Jews and pagans. Betraying his negus, he proclaimed himself king of southern Arabia. A Nestorian Christian, he decided to conquer northern Arabia, both to enlarge his holdings and to end the rites at Mecca, the leading pagan sanctuary. He began by preventing his own followers from making the annual pilgrimage, in response to which a Bedouin defiled the cathedral of Qullays, which Abraha had had built at Sanaa, capital of his kingdom.

To avenge this outrage, Abraha, mounted atop an elephant brought for that purpose from Africa, led his army against Mecca. Muslim exegetes relate that

Above: Scene of daily life in a caravansary from a Turkish miniature.
Below: House in Mecca.

Opposite: Remains of a house in Medina dating to the period of Muhammad's father, Abdullah.

when the army came within sight of Mecca, "The elephant knelt and refused to go forward; then a swarm of birds flew over the army holding stones in their beaks and talons that they let fall on the soldiers; and the soldiers when struck died." The Koran relates (105): *Have you not seen how the Lord dealt with the elephant people? Did he not bring their stratagem to naught and send against them birds in flocks? Clay-stones did they hurl down upon them, and he made them like stubble eaten down by cattle.*

Scholars have theorized that this refers to an outbreak of smallpox that took place at precisely the right moment. That day was September 1, 570;

of which is the *Sahih* (The Authentic), compiled and edited by the Arabic scholar al-Bukhari (d. 870). The other biographical texts were written one or two hundred years after Muhammad's death, such as the *Sira* and the *Maghazi* written by Ibn Ishaq (d. 768). There are then the texts that contain "traditions" attributed to contemporaries, in particular the *Ta'rikh al-Rusul wa al-Muluk* by the Persian al-Tabari (d. 922). Even so, while the date of birth may be reasonable, the attack on Mecca led by Abraha almost certainly took place quite a bit earlier.

Muhammad's father was called Abdullah (Servant of Allah), although many scholars believe the name to be posthumous. He belonged to the Banu Hashim clan, which had the privilege of distributing water from the Zamzam fountain to pilgrims. He died during a business trip to Medina (then called Yathrib), a few months before the birth of Muhammad. Muhammad's mother, Amina bint Wahb ibn Abd Manaaf, was the daughter of the head of the Banu

the same day, according to Muslim hagiography, as the birth of Muhammad. No sources exist to confirm the date of his birth with absolute certainty, nor is there any truly unquestionable information concerning the earliest years of his life. The fact remains that Muhammad is a pre-Islamic name; in his youth he was also called al-Amin (The Trustworthy One), perhaps a nickname, and also Mustafa, a name later preferred by many Turkish poets.

The question of sources is of importance. The essential source for Muhammad's life is without doubt the Koran, at least in terms of the period of his preaching. There is then the information found in the "sayings," also called the "Tradition," the Hadith; these are collections of statements attributed to the Prophet, to members of his family, or to his companions. There are four main collections of these, among the best

Left: Muhammad's mother showing him to his grandfather Abd al-Muttalib in an eighteenth-century Turkish miniature; Topkapi Palace Library, Istanbul.

Opposite top: The "pool" of Abraham at Ur of the Chaldeans.

Opposite bottom: The young Muhammad being interrogated by the Christian monk Bahira; fourteenth-century Iranian miniature, University Library, Edinburgh.

Zahra in Medina. Thus, even before his birth, Muhammad had close ties to the city that was destined to be of primary importance to the future of Islam, a fact that has never been given importance by biographers.

In keeping with custom, his paternal grandfather, Abd al-Muttalib, assumed parental authority of the orphan. Also in keeping with custom, his mother entrusted the boy to a black wet nurse for a month and then, when the tribe of the Banu Sa'd came to Mecca for the ritual annual pilgrimage, to a wet nurse of that people, Halima bint Abi Dhu'ayd.

Thus Muhammad left the city and spent five years as a nomad in the desert between the oasis of Ta'if and Mecca, enjoying the freedom of life among the tribe of Bedouins reputed to speak the purest Arabic. It was during this period, perhaps the most carefree of his life, that Muslim exegetes, referring to Koran 94:1–3, locate a hagiographic event that is open to a variety of interpretations. According to the Koran:

Have we not opened thine heart for thee? And taken off from thee thy burden, which galled thy back? On the basis of this, some early writers claimed that the child Muhammad had truly been grasped by two angels that opened his chest and removed a black lump from his heart. Perhaps this was an act of purification that should be compared to the concept of "original sin," which is so important to Christianity but is completely absent from Islam. The other verses of the sura suggest a more symbolic and moral meaning.

Victor Hugo

"O leader of the believers! As soon as you understood, the world believed in your word. The day in which you were born a star appeared, and three towers in the palace of Khorsu collapsed!"
Victor Hugo
(1802–1885),
La Légende des Siècles,
IX, Islam

"The Trustworthy One"

When he was six, Muhammad returned to Mecca, an event that may very well have been his first experience of sorrow, a result of detachment from his wet nurse and from the carefree life he had been living during the years that modern psychology sees as the most important in terms of mental formation.

According to certain hagiographic sources—but such sources agree on few points concerning Muhammad's early childhood—a few months after his return, his mother took him to Yathrib (Medina) to visit some relatives. On the return trip, at Abwa, she died. So it was that Muhammad began the difficult life of an orphan, made only harder by a society based on property and commerce. This has furnished psychologists with abundant material concerning the formation of the character and personality of Muhammad. In fact, throughout his life Muhammad paid special attention to the care of orphans and the disinherited, people given no status in pre-Islamic Mecca. The Koran itself has many

passages in their defense and has words of violent condemnation for the selfish and the dishonest.

Similar life events very often contribute to the formation of a weak and introspective character, whereas Muhammad demonstrated a strong, open, loyal, creative, and balanced character, free of psychological dysfunctions even in the most difficult moments.

The orphan was taken in by his grandfather Abd

al-Muttalib, born in Yathrib, but two years later, he too died. The young Muhammad then went to live with his paternal uncle Abu Talib, who raised him as his own son, taking him along on his caravan all the way to Palestine and Syria—at least so claims hagiography, but Western scholars express doubts. Muhammad would have seen the great Byzantine churches and monasteries and also, along the caravan route, the ruins of the great cities of the past of which the Koran speaks (15:74–84), Madian, Hedjr, Sodom, Gomorrah: *And we*

turned the city upside down, and we rained stones of baked clay upon them. Verily, in this are signs for those who scan heedfully; and these cities lay on the high road. Verily, in this are signs for the faithful. The inhabitants also of El Aika [Madian] were sinners.

It seems that in the course of one of these trips with his uncle, Muhammad, by then nine or twelve, went to Bosra in Syria, where he met a Christian monk named Bahira (Aramaic *bekhira*: "the elect"), a scholar of scriptures who, according to Islamic hagiography, recognized Muhammad as the Prophet announced in the Bible. For several centuries, the Byzantines, seeking to discredit Islam, wrote that the monk was a Nestorian, author of a heretical *Apocalypse* (which survives in Arabic and Syriac), and that it was he who suggested to Muhammad many holy stories later reported in the Koran; this seems improbable, given that it was a very short visit.

Every year the young Muhammad attended the great fair at Ukad, in which Arabs from across the

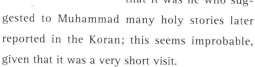

peninsula participated, along with many foreigners, most of all Syrians, Persians, and Indians. Poets vied for the best epic, seers chanted rhythmic spells, sports champions competed. There was much commercial activity, but also a great exchange of religious and cultural ideas. Muhammad must also have experienced some of the Sacrilegious War (*Harb al-Fijar*), so called because it was fought in sacred months, the second war between Mecca and the Hawazin Bedouins, which went on for nearly five years.

A child of his environment and a participant in the various cultures that surrounded Arabia Felix, Muhammad spent this period of his life traveling the great caravan routes of the incense trade, eventually becoming himself the leader of a caravan. Because of all the many dangers and responsibilities inherent in the post, leading a caravan was an undertaking that required an intelligent, strong, and also quick-witted man. It was rare to find a leader who, in addition to these qualities, was also scrupulously honest, but such was the case with Muhammad, so much so that his contemporaries nicknamed him al-Amin: "The Trustworthy One."

One of Muhammad's distant cousins, Khadija (daughter of Kuwaylid of the Asad of the Quraysh clan of Mecca, widow of the wealthy Utayyiq), noticed him and entrusted him with a caravan to Bosra. When Muhammad returned from this mission, the two decided to marry. When the marriage contract was signed, Khadija was legally represented by her uncle Amr ibn Asa, and Muhammad by his uncle Hamza.

According to the scholar al-Tabari, Muhammad and Khadija had four sons: Abdullah, al-Qasim, al-Tahir, and al-Tayyb, all of whom died at a young age; and four daughters: Zaynab, Rukayya, Umm Kulthum, and the best known of them, Fatima. The wise Khadija and the generous Muhammad also adopted a slave child that they freed, Zayd ibn Haritha, but he too died—in battle—at a young age.

So it was that at just over twenty-five, Muhammad, an orphan without status in a society that put its highest value on possessions, found himself in a good social position thanks to possessions, to which he added, however, his outstanding moral and intellectual qualities, which all those around him recognized and valued.

Opposite top: *Syrian Arabs Traveling* (detail), by Prosper Marilhat (1811–1847).

Opposite bottom: The marriage of Muhammad and Khadija in an eighteenth-century Turkish miniature.

Above: The Prophet and Khadija, perhaps while he was serving as her camel driver (the scene is given various interpretations) in an eighteenth-century Turkish miniature, Topkapi Palace Library, Istanbul.

MUHAMMAD REBUILDS THE KA'BA

Ten years went by, of which Muslim hagiography says nothing. Muhammad presumably ran his wife's business and saw to his family. An event then occurred whose importance is recognized by all Islamic historians.

The Ka'ba is the most important, famous, and sacred sanctuary of Islam. According to the Koran (2:121–127), it was erected by the patriarch Abraham with the help of his firstborn son, Ishmael. Located at the center of the courtyard of the mosque of Mecca, it owes its name to its nearly cubic shape; in fact, it measures fifty feet in height, three of its sides are roughly thirty feet high, and the facade, which faces northeast, is about thirty-five feet wide. Such are the measurements of the most recent version, for over the course of the centuries, the building has gone through a variety of appearances, primarily as a result of

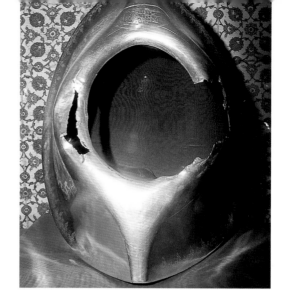

Above: Ancient gold frame for the Black Stone of the Ka'ba, pavilion of the Holy Mantle, Topkapi Palace Museum, Istanbul.
Below: Contemporary view of the courtyard of the sanctuary of Mecca with the Ka'ba at the center.

Opposite top: Bizighurmud and the horoscope, from the *Khamsa* by Nizami, Shiraz, 1491, National Library, St. Petersburg.
Opposite bottom: Map showing the Ka'ba and the divisions of the various parts of the world from a seventeenth-century Iraqi miniature.

political events. On the left side of its facade, about six feet from the ground, is the only door. The corners are directed toward the four cardinal points; in the one facing east, at a height of about five feet, is inserted the Black Stone. There are those who believe it to be a meteorite; others believe it to be a very dark porphyry. It no longer has its original angular shape but has been convexly hollowed out by the kisses given it over the centuries by thousands of pilgrims. About fourteen inches in diameter, it is framed by a wide silver band. A far older, gold frame is today in the pavilion of the Holy Mantle of the Topkapi Palace Museum, named for a mantle that belonged to Muhammad. Also on display are Muhammad's bow and sword, a letter he wrote, and other reliquaries, both his and from the four "rightly guided" caliphs. In the opposite corner of the Ka'ba, at the same height as the Black Stone, is another angular stone, a reddish one known as the *alhajar alas'ad*, "the stone of felicity," which pilgrims touch, believing it brings good luck.

The four walls of the Ka'ba are of a stone quarried in the mountains surrounding Mecca. They are covered by a large black cloth, with gold and silver embroidery along the entire upper part at two-thirds of its height. This is the *kiswa*: every year since the thirteenth century a new one has been provided by Egypt, since following the annual pilgrimage it is cut into pieces that are sold to the faithful by the Banu Shayba. This is by no means the only way in which the Saudis profit from the religious fervor of the pilgrims.

The single door to the Ka'ba is decorated with silver in some places and gold in others, contravening orthodox Islam, which recommends against the use of gold and silver for religious activities. When the door is open, a wheeled, wooden staircase is leaned against it, making it possible to enter the Ka'ba. Inside, three wooden columns support the flat roof, which can be reached by a flight of stairs. The floor is of marble, and from the ceiling hang gold and silver lamps. Tablets on the rear wall record the reconstructions and restorations of the building. The original structure was probably made primarily of wood, with a door at ground level.

When Muhammad had been married ten years, a powerful storm damaged the building. The four leading tribes of Mecca agreed that each would rebuild one side of the building, but they almost came to blows over which had the right to put the Black Stone in place. They decided to give the decision to the next person to enter the sacred space: that person was Muhammad. The decision he reached displays his great sagacity: he placed the stone at the center of a large blanket and had one representative from each of the four tribes take hold of a corner. They then lifted the blanket and carried the stone at the necessary height. When the moment came, Muhammad placed it in position. When this had been done, the wise judgment of this honest man was once again praised.

The Night of Destiny

Not everyone was pleased with the paganism of the commercial hierarchy of Mecca. Some, seeking an intimate and pure religion, found themselves in opposition to the prevailing polytheism. These people, called *hunafa* (singular *hanif*), considered themselves followers of the true monotheistic word of the patriarch Abraham. When he was nearing forty, Muhammad too began to sense increasing longing for a divine identity. He began taking long, solitary walks in the desert surrounding Mecca, out among the mountains and rocks. On occasion he withdrew for several days at a time on Mount Abu Qubays, spending as long as a month in a cave in Mount Hira, today known as Jabal al-Nur, "the Mountain of Light." It was here, on the night of the twenty-seventh day of Ramadan in the year 612, that he had a vision. The "Sayings of the Prophet" collected in the *Sahih* by the Arabic scholar Muhammad al-Bukhari provide a description from a "witness" of the time: "Urwa ibn al-Zubair recounts that Aisha, wife of the Prophet, said: The Messenger of God began to have pious visions during his sleep. Each

of those visions appeared to him like the break of day. After this, solitude became dear to him, and he went to a cave on Hira to practice the *tahannuth*. The *tahannuth* consisted of reciting prayers for a certain number of nights before returning to his

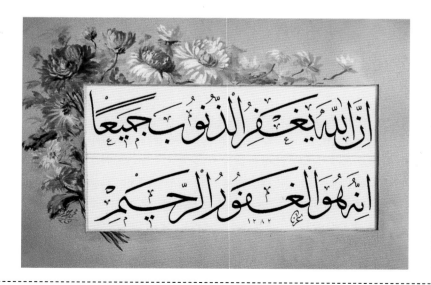

Opposite: The Ka'ba from the Pushtu *Anthology* of the Hetimandel princes, 1520, State Library, Kabul, Afghanistan.

Above: *Simurgh Carrying the Infant Zal to Its Nest*, from a *Shahnama*, Tabriz, ca. 1370, Topkapi Palace Library, Istanbul.

Left: Invocation to God, pardoner of all sins, in nineteenth-century Ottoman calligraphy, Topkapi Palace Library, Istanbul.

صودن ایجدی کوردیکم اولصو قاردن صووق شکردن شربند داول اوغازل
ایتدی یا محمد شبدی بلدمکه سنك الله تعالی قتنه قربك واردر

منزلك عظیم ایمثر دعاك مستجاب بابش امایا محمد بنم ایكی درلو حاجتم
دخی واردردار اکر اولایکی درلو حاجتمی روا قلورسك اولایکی کسوکوم

let go, saying, "Recite!" "I am not one of those that recite," I answered again. And again he took me, for the third time, and held me so hard that I could no longer stand it, then he let go, saying: *Recite, in the name of thy Lord who created, who created man from a clot of blood. Recite, for thy lord is the most beneficent, who hath taught the use of the pen, hath taught man that which he kneweth not*' " (Koran 96:1–5).

"The Messenger of God returned home with these verses, taken with a great trembling, and when he reached Khadija he told her, 'I am cold, cover me!' When he was covered his panic passed away. Then, turning to his wife, he said, 'O Khadija, I am afraid for my life,' and he told her what had happened. She responded, 'No, be happy, give glory to God. God never inflicts humiliation. In the name of God you will join relatives, will speak the truth, help the afflicted, give to the poor, ensure hospitality to the guest, and help us face the vicissitudes of fate.'

"Khadija took him to see Waraqa ibn Naufal, the son of her father's brother. He was a man who at the time of paganism had converted to Christianity and had made a written Arabic translation of the part of the Gospel that God had wanted. An

family. He took provisions and then returned to Khadija to get more until the day when the Truth came to him while he was in the cave of Hira. An angel appeared and said, 'Recite!' 'I am not one of those that recite,' responded the Messenger of God. 'Then'—he recounted—'the angel took me and held me so hard I could no longer breathe. Then he let go, saying, "Recite!" "I am not one of those that recite," I responded again. He took me again, a second time, and held me so that I could no longer breathe, then

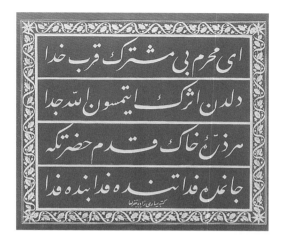

soon after, and the revelation was interrupted, for which the Messenger of God was very saddened."

These are the "sayings" of the companions of the Prophet and of the Prophet himself. There is a marked difference between the simple style of these works and the fluent style of the Koran.

Bukhari's book continues: "Jabir ibn Abdallah refers that the Messenger of God, speaking of the interruption of the revelation, said, 'While we walked, I heard a voice that came from the sky. I lifted my eyes and saw the Angel that had come to find me at Hira. He was seated on a throne between the sky and the earth. I went away from him and went home, saying, "I am very cold, cover me."'" When the Prophet was covered God revealed these words to him: *O thou, enveloped in the cloak, Arise and warn! Magnify thy lord. Purify thy raiment. Flee all that angers God* (Koran 74:1–5). 'What angers God,' said Abu Salama, 'means the idols that the pagans worshipped.' Now the revelations continued without interruption."

Opposite: The Prophet Muhammad speaking with a monotheistic shepherd in an eighteenth-century Turkish miniature, Topkapi Palace Library, Istanbul.

Quatrain (*top*) and poem (*above*) in praise of the Prophet Muhammad.

Right: Muttalin and Abd al-Muttalid arrive in Mecca, eighteenth-century Turkish miniature.

elderly man, he had become blind.

"'Uncle,' Khadija said to him, 'listen to your brother's son.' 'O son of my brother,' asked Waraqa, 'what do you see?' The Prophet told him of his visions. Waraqa said, 'This is the Namus that was revealed to Moses. Ah, if only I were still young! If only I could still be living when your people drive you out!' The Messenger of God asked, 'Will they drive me out?' 'Yes,' responded Waraqa, 'No man who has brought what you bring has ever failed to be persecuted. If I am still alive in that moment I will help you with all my strength.' But Waraqa died

The Wives of Muhammad

The first wife was Khadija, daughter of Kuwaylid of the Meccan clan of the Asad Quraysh. She had already had two husbands: Abu Hala al-Tamimi, from whom she was divorced, and Utayyik ibn Aidh, who had died. She was forty (some sources say twenty-eight) when she married Muhammad, who was twenty-three. They had four daughters (Zaynab, Rukayya, Umm Kulthum, and Fatima) and four sons (Abdullah, al-Qasim, al-Tahir, and al-Tayyb), all of

Below: The wives of the Prophet Muhammad in an eighteenth-century Turkish miniature, Topkapi Palace Library, Istanbul.

Opposite top: Khadija sees the young Muhammad returning from his first trip, miniature from the *History* by Ishak of Nishapur, 1581.

Safiya bint Huyayy; Maymuna bint al-Harit of the Hilal; Zaynab bint Jahsh of the Banu Asad, who divorced Zayd to marry Muhammad, of whom she seems to have been deeply enamored; and a Banu Mustaliq, Juwayriyya bint al-Harith. After 627 he married a freed Coptic slave, Marya, who gave him a son, Ibrahim, who died at about two. He also married other women, according to political necessity and the customs of the time, in order to make blood ties to Bedouin tribes. The subject of the number of Muhammad's wives, still discussed, has been studied in depth by the traditionalist Abu Abd-Allah Saad (784–845) in *Kitab al-Tabaqut al-Kabir*, an edition of which was printed in Beirut in 1958.

Below: The wives of the Prophet, fifteenth-century Iranian ceramic.

whom died young. Muhammad's second wife—after Khadija died—was Sawda bint Zama'a, the thirty-year-old widow of a Muslim who had emigrated to Abyssinia. Muhammad married her when he arrived in Medina. The third was Aisha, daughter of Abu Bakr, the youngest and the only one of his wives—not having been previously married—who was still a virgin when they married. Then came Hafsa, the sister or daughter (according to some sources) of Umar ibn al-Khattab (successor to Muhammad as the second caliph); Umm Habiba, daughter of Abu Sufyan, head of the Meccans; and Umm Salama, daughter of Abu Umayya. All these women were Quraysh. He also married a Jew of Khaybar named

The "Descent" of the First Revelation

So it was that the first revelation occurred; so it was that the first verses of the Koran "descended" on Muhammad.

It meant enlightenment and the understanding—as well as the anguish—of his mission. It is a state well known to poets and prophets who, when in the thrall of inspiration, write things without any awareness of what they are writing; they write things that they themselves could never have imagined being able to write as much as a moment before. A psychoanalyst could attempt a plausible analysis: Muhammad was truly in an unnatural state, but at the same time, and in the most certain sense, it was not a paranoid state. In simple terms, this was not a matter of a vision or a mystification, but rather a hyperperceptive man experiencing an honest inspiration. To understand it would require exper-

Above: Modern allegory of Muhammad's moment of inspiration.

Below: Page of the *Mathnawi* by Jalal al-Din Rumi (1207–1273) that exalts the moment of inspiration, Konya, Turkey.

Opposite top: Description of the "mystic state" in a Sufi manuscript, Tashkent, Uzbekistan.

Opposite bottom: Exaltation of the Night of Destiny, fifteenth-century Iranian ceramic.

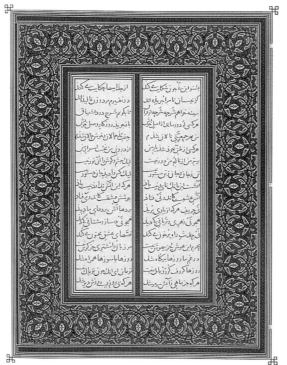

iments with the states of poetic inspiration or the hypersensitivity of a seer or the enormously heightened awareness of the tangible world experienced by a condemned man during the last moments of his life—any one of which might provide a sense of the state of mind in which Muhammad must have found himself when he was inspired and a section of the Koran "descended" over him. Only those who have experienced one of the above-cited psychic states (rather than "spiritual," so as to remain within the field of provable facts, of the perceptible) can accept and testify to the true force of inspiration that is meant, which is by no means to be confused with any kind of mystification.

One might consider the accounts left by Muhammad's contemporaries who were present during those moments to be less than trustworthy; after all, some of them were blinded by enthusiasm or fanaticism.

But the words with which they described Muhammad's "ecstatic states" support the authenticity of his inspirations. In another passage of his collection, Bukhari states: "When a revelation descended on the Prophet he perspired, even in cold weather"; Ibn Saad writes that "the Prophet weighed so much at those times that if he was on his camel it crouched." In another place Bukhari cites the report of a companion who said, "One day I was standing beside him in a room that was so full of people that his thigh touched me. Suddenly the state of revelation took him and I felt his tremendous weight break my femur." Similar states have been experienced by mystics of many religions, and they have left reliably objective descriptions of them. There are then the great Sufi masters for whom such states are common, have been described in depth, and are achievable by those of their students who reach a profound enough understanding of their teaching.

The fact remains that the fateful night of the first revelation is still celebrated today with prayers and readings of the Koran by all Muslims. The Koran itself says (97): *Verily, we have caused it to descend on the night of power. And who shall teach thee what the night of power is? The night of power is more beautiful than a thousand months; therein descend the angels and the spirit by permission of their Lord for every matter. A night of peace until the rising of the dawn.*

As for the affirmation of Waraqa, son of Naufal, the elderly blind Christian, with his deep knowledge of the Scriptures ("In truth Muhammad is the awaited Prophet, the Paraclete"), this expresses a concept dear to Muslims and repeated in the Koran (61:6; also 26:196). As early as the eighth century, Ibn Ishaq cited the Gospel of John (16:7–14) in which Jesus says, "Nevertheless I tell you the truth; It is expedient for you that I go away: for if I go not away, the Comforter [in the original Greek, *Parakletos*, meaning "worthy of praise," or, in Arabic, *Muhammad*] will not come unto you; but if I depart, I will send him unto you. And when he is come, he will reprove the world of sin, and of right-

eousness, and of judgment ... when he, the Spirit of truth, is come, he will guide you into all truth: for he shall not speak of himself; but whatsoever he shall hear, that shall he speak; and he will show you things to come. He shall glorify me: for he shall receive of mine, and shall show it unto you."

In discussing this biblical verse, Islamic scholars compare it to other texts. The *Zand Avesta* of Zoroastrianism says: "An iconoclast who will be called 'the one worthy of praise,' mercy on all" (13, XXVIII:129); the Brahmanic Vedas predict "a wise man will arrive in the desert, called 'the worthy of praise,' an owner of camels, one of whose victories will be won with three hundred armed men and one with a thousand." The *Kalnki Purana* announces, "A divine incarnation whose father will be called 'slave of God,' his mother 'worthy of faith.' He will be born in the land of sand and will have to seek refuge to the north of the city of his birth."

Thomas Carlyle

"The lies, which well-meaning zeal has heaped around this man, are disgraceful to ourselves only ... The word this man spoke has been the life-guidance now to a hundred and eighty millions of men ... such a man is what we call an original man; he comes to us first-hand. A messenger he, sent from the Infinite Unknown with tidings to us."
Thomas Carlyle (1795–1881),
On Heroes, Hero Worship and the Heroic in History

THE YEAR OF SORROW

For the first three years Muhammad preached the abandonment to a single God and the condemnation of polytheism only to his family, including Khadija, Abu Bakr, Ali, Waraqa, son of Naufal, Zayd ibn Harita, Abi Quhafa, and others. He then began to preach in public, reciting the verses that were being revealed to him in the open area near the Ka'ba. At first he was mocked, but the opposition steadily grew more forceful. His new, simple religion spread most of all among women, Christians, slaves, and the underprivileged; even so, it would be wrong to think it had the characteristics of a proletarian movement. Instances of important Quraysh embracing Islam were rare during this period. Among the few were Muhammad's uncle Hamza ibn Abd al-Muttalib and Umar, son of Khattab, both regarded as fierce men whose conversions were thus all the more remarkable.

Muhammad's teaching was clear, slow, and simple, and its markedly monotheistic aspects were abundantly clear, but his message was not limited to the religious sphere. For example, there had been much discussion in Mecca of the victory won by the Sassanid Khosru II, king of Persia—and thus a worshipper of idols—over the Byzantine emperor Heraclius in 614. Khosru II had occupied Syria and Egypt, destroying churches and profaning and sacking the Holy Sepulcher. The Meccans sided with Khosru and were pleased by his victory; the early Muslims, feeling a closer affinity to Christian monotheism, were saddened by the event. The Koran (30:2–5) states:

The Greeks have been defeated in a land hard by; but after their defeat they shall defeat their foes, in a few years. First and last is the affair with God. And on that day shall the faithful rejoice. It is the promise of God: to his promise God will not be untrue; but most men know it not.

Believing in this prediction, Abu Bakr bet the Quraysh a hundred camels and won the bet in 625 when Heraclius defeated the Sassanids, drove them

Opposite top: Exaltation of Muhammad's revelation, portal of the Ince Minare madrasa, Konya, Turkey.

Opposite bottom: A Muslim mystic in a cave, miniature from the *Mier Musawwir*,

ca. 1535, British Museum, London.

Right: Footprint of the Prophet Muhammad, pavilion of the Holy Mantle, Topkapi Palace Museum, Istanbul.

عاد قوم هلاك قلد وم مسنك دوشمنلروكى دخى شوبله هلواد
قلائمرددى اندن رسول عليه السلام اول برسى دخى ايزو

اوفدى ايتدى سنينه مؤكل سنددى اول فرشته دخى ايتك
بن دكر لرصولرا وستنه موكم حق تعالى بلوندن ابن بقصورو

him. Against him "descended" Sura 111, the sixth in the chronological order, with five verses: *Let the hands of Abu Lahab perish, and let himself perish! His wealth and his gains shall avail him not. Burned shall he be at the fiery flame, and his wife laden with firewood, on her neck a rope of palm fiber.*

But the year of sorrow arrived. In 620 Muhammad's wife Khadija died, as did his uncle and protector Abu Talib, head of the Hashim clan. As though to complete Muhammad's undoing, his uncle Abu Lahab became the clan leader and made peace with the Quraysh by disowning the Prophet. In the customs of the time, Muhammad found himself more or less isolated, deprived of the protection of his clan. Only the ongoing revelations sustained and reassured him.

Faced with the Meccan hostility, Muhammad sought allies among the Bedouins, who repaid him with treachery and betrayal. When he appealed to the inhabitants of the oasis of Ta'if, they responded by nearly stoning him to death—he was saved by

from the occupied territories, and invaded Persia, achieving a great victory at Nineveh.

Muhammad had to face increasing hostility. The idea of worshipping only one God went against the pagan interests of the Quraysh, and Muhammad spoke out against their immoral ways with fiery words. Muhammad was mocked, sometimes violently, and professional poets declaimed satires against him. The situation became so tense that those among the converts who lacked political "backing" or influential friends were forced to secretly emigrate to Ethiopia. In the end, the Quraysh threatened to exile the clan of the Hashim, and the men who had married Muhammad's daughters repudiated them. Among these was Utba, son of Abu Lahab. Abu Lahab himself (Abd al Uzza, later called Abu Lahab, "Father of Flame"), although an uncle of the Prophet, fiercely opposed

Opposite top: The journey to heaven of the Prophet Muhammad, eighteenth-century Turkish miniature, Topkapi Palace Library, Istanbul.

Opposite bottom: The journey to heaven of the Prophet Muhammad, *Uigur Mi'raj-Nameh* of the fourteenth century, National Library, Paris.

Right: The Night Journey, or Ascent, of the Prophet Muhammad, replica of a miniature from a *Kitab al-Mir'aj* by Lassaad al-Karqi, ca. 1520, private collection, Kabul.

taking refuge in a garden tended by Christian slaves. He was able to return to Mecca thanks to the protection of a valiant man, Mutim, son of Adi.

During this period of discouragement, an event occurred that the Koran (17:1) writes off in a few words: *Glory be to him who carried his servant by night from the sacred temple of Mecca to the temple that is more remote, whose precinct we have blessed, that we might show him of our signs.*

On the twenty-seventh day of the month of Ramadan in the year 620, Muhammad slept in the home of his cousin Umm Hani, daughter of Abu Talib, and had a vision in which the angel Gabriel took him on a celestial ride. "Flying" on a winged beast called the Buraq, he went from the Ka'ba to the Temple of Jerusalem, then on to Sinai and Bethlehem. He met Abraham, Moses, and Jesus; rising into the seven heavens along a ladder (*mi'raj*) of light, he met other prophets. The trip became increasingly symbolic. The *Sahih* by Bukhari (LXIII:40) includes an abundant description of it.

There are four principal versions of the Night Journey (*Kitab al-Mir'aj*), along with various secondary ones—according to a theory proposed by the Spanish Jesuit Asin Palacios in 1919, Dante got the idea for his *Divine Comedy* from a Provençal version. In time, the Night Journey came to be looked upon by certain Islamic fundamentalists as an event that had actually taken place, but most serious Muslim scholars, such as Tabari (d. 923), Razi (d. 1210), and Ghazali (the "Master of the Masters," 1050–1111), thought the trip was also open to a symbolic interpretation as a sort of mystical-contemplative ascent, thus leading to numerous Sufi exegeses. Tabari (XV:17) wrote: "His spirit took this trip, but in his drowsy state it seemed to the Prophet to actually travel bodily, riding a horse. The apparent movement expressed by the words relate in effect to the lifting away of veils that prevent our physical natures from perceiving divine reality."

While popular piety may attribute various miracles to Muhammad, serious historians do not, preferring to keep the figure of the great Prophet within the limits of human reality, even if he was the man "chosen by God."

THE "EMIGRATION" TO MEDINA

The Quraysh were casting about for a way to kill Muhammad without incurring the tribal laws of retaliation and blood feud. The inhabitants of Yathrib, however, most particularly the Arab tribes of the Aws and Khazraj, listened to Muhammad's preaching and responded well to him, seeing him as someone capable of acting as an arbiter of peace (*sayyd*) among the local Arabic, Jewish, and Christian tribes. In fact, a large group of Catholic Christians had taken refuge in Yathrib, fleeing the recent persecu-

tions directed against them by the Byzantine Christians to the north. Their arrival in the city had upset the local balance. At the same time, old rancor had burst out in a sort of battle fought around 617 at a place called Bu'ath. The fight had resolved nothing. The city was in need of a kind of impartial judge, and by then Muhammad's fairness had become proverbial.

During the annual pilgrimage in 620, six members of the Khazraj tribe met with Muhammad. During the next year's pilgrimage, representatives of both the Aws and the Khazraj made a secret pact with Muhammad, and this became a formal agreement in June 622, again during the pilgrimage, when seventy-five citizens of Yathrib met with Muhammad at Aqaba, not far from Mecca, and swore themselves to him.

The agreement made Muhammad director of the political affairs of the city and gave him the freedom to preach what he believed. In response, the Muslims of Mecca began an exodus to Yathrib, such that eventually only the Prophet, Abu Bakr (a rich man destined to be a leading figure in the later development of Islam), and perhaps also Ali were left. On Friday, July 16, 622 (according to

وزلدى ذوق وصفا لراولدى اولولق حرمتي تمام ُيرينه كليد

وكز مدينه يهوديلرينه خبر اولدى انلردخى باشقه برجماعت

Islamic hagiography; some historians put the date sixty-eight days later because of the discrepancy between the lunar and solar calendars), the Prophet was alerted that the Quraysh were about to make an attempt on his life. Together with his trusted friend Abu Bakr, he fled the city. The Meccans searched for them, but in vain, for the two were hiding in a cave on Mount Thawr, as related in the Koran (9:40): *Allah helped him formerly, when the unbelievers drove him forth, in the company of a second only! When they two were in the cave; when the Prophet said to his companion, "Be not distressed; verily, God is with us."*

A spider quickly spun a large web at the opening to the cave that fooled the enemies when they passed·by. Then the Prophet and Abu Bakr, using little-known paths and with the timely assistance of a Bedouin guide and a freed slave, Amir ibn Fuhayra, escaped the searchers and, despite the bounty on their heads (one hundred camels), made

the town of Medina was receptive to the religious concepts preached by Muhammad; nor was it the site of an annual pilgrimage with special interests to safeguard; what it needed instead was a sort of governor-peacemaker. Muhammad thus became the town's moderator, but as indicated by the Koran (4: 59–60), he did not easily become its spiritual leader. Reading between the lines, one realizes that in Yathrib he soon came up against the insolent and quibbling nature of the Jewish clans,

The Changes of Medina

When he first arrived in Medina, Muhammad tried to win the favor of the Jewish clans with a series of compromises, but did not succeed. Some Western scholars see this as the reason for the progressive pan-Arabian consolidation of Islam. Between 623 and 624 the qibla (the direction in which the faithful faces in prayer) was changed. The Christians turned to the east, the Jews, Ebionites, Elkesaites, and others faced toward Jerusalem, as did the Muslims originally; but now verses 136–150 of the second sura changed the direction of the qibla, turning Muslims toward the Ka'ba (in all mosques this direction is indicated by a more or less elaborately decorated niche, the mihrab, located on the wall toward Mecca). Another break was the later refusal by the Muslims to hold that God rested after the six days of Creation. There was then the institution of the fast in the month of Ramadan, somewhat analogous to the Jewish Yom Kippur and the Christian Lent; and finally the designation "Muslim" given to Abraham, first true hanif (monotheist; follower of the original religion of God).

it safe and sound to Yathrib on September 24, 622.

This was the "emigration," in Arabic *hijra*, hence in English "hegira" or "hejira," meaning "flight."

From that date begins the computation of time according to the Muslim calendar, with AH, from the Latin *Anno Hejirae*, replacing AD. Being based on the phases of the moon rather than the cycle of the sun, the Muslim year is $\frac{1}{33}$ shorter than the solar year.

A few years after the hegira the name of the town of Yathrib changed, becoming the "City of the Prophet" (*madinat al-Nabi*, hence Medina). Most of all because of the presence of monotheistic Jews,

observed those to whom a part of the Scriptures hath been given? They believe in Djibt and Thagout, and say of the infidels, "These are guided in a better path than those who hold the faith." These are they whom God hath cursed.

THE VICTORY AT BADR

A few months after setting himself up at Medina, Muhammad sent a contingent under Abd-Allah ibn Jahsh to Nakhla to attack a small Quraysh caravan that believed itself immune to attack because it was traveling in the sacred month of Rajab. There were few defenders, victory was easily won, and spoils were plentiful. These spoils (the tribal system of the time saw such spoils as a legal means of earning wealth) were needed to nourish the Emigrants. In this small way began the series of roughly eighty military campaigns against the Quraysh, the

which were hardly disposed to accept him as a "prophet." Even so, as soon as he arrived he had Islam's first mosque built, a refuge for the persecuted, a court, the headquarters of his "council of state." He divided the townspeople into two groups, the Emigrants (*Muhajirun*, the fugitives from Mecca, more of whom continued to arrive) and the Helpers (*Ansar*, the neo-Muslims of Medina).

Two leaders of the Jewish Banu Qaynuqa clan—Akhtab and Ashraf—went to Mecca to make an alliance with the Quraysh against Muhammad. To test their sincerity, the Meccans asked them to kneel before the idols Djibt and Thagout, which they willingly did. The Koran (4:54) states: *Hast thou not*

Opposite: The arrival of the Prophet in Medina, miniature from Lahore (Punjab), ca. 1800. Above: One of the oldest houses in the city of Medina. Right: Remains of a fortified house of the Banu Qaynuqa near Medina.

Jewish clans, the Bedouin tribes, and finally the Byzantine garrisons on the northwestern frontier that ended with the final victory of Islam.

A little later (in the month of Ramadan, AH 2: March 624) Muhammad organized a small force of about three hundred men and led it himself in an attack on a Meccan caravan from Syria guided by Abu Sufyan and defended by about 950 armed men under the command of Abu Jahal, a former childhood friend of Muhammad. Born in 570, head of

Above: Idealization of the hero in battle, miniature from Tabriz, ca. 1345, Museum of Fine Arts, Boston.

Left: Tomb built on the site of the battle of Badr.

Opposite: The Prophet Muhammad faces a superior number of enemy troops, eighteenth-century Turkish miniature, Topkapi Palace Library, Istanbul.

the Makhzum after the death of al-Walid ibn al-Mughira, he had incited the Hashim against the early Muslims. The encounter took place near Badr Hunayn, to the southwest of Medina. About seventy of the Quraysh, including Abu Jahal, died in the battle, while only fifteen Muslims died. The victors brought many prisoners back to Medina, along with abundant spoils that were divided among all the Muslims. A few years later the mother of Abu Jahal, Asma bint Mukharriba, converted to Islam; she died in around 636.

The victory at Badr increased Muhammad's prestige. On his return to Medina, he dealt with the Jewish Banu Qaynuqa clan. Because of the pact they had made with the Meccans, he ordered them to either convert or leave. They rejected this proposal, and on April 1, 624, Muhammad and a hundred men laid siege to the clan's fort. After fifteen days, the clan capitulated. Muhammad ordered them to leave, allowing them to take with them whatever a camel could carry for every two families. All of the Banu Qaynuqa sought refuge in Syria, except for two families that preferred to emigrate to Khaybar and a

woman who married the Prophet. By then Muhammad was fifty-four and had ten wives, five of them Quraysh, one a Jew of Khaybar, a Hilal, an Asad, and a Mustaliq. He was later to marry a Copt named Marya. Of all of these, only the youngest, Aisha, daughter of Abu Bakr, was neither widowed nor divorced. Later on, Islamic law notably changed the condition of women and their situation in marriage compared to the customs of the *jahiliyya* (the age of ignorance and barbarities, the pre-Islamic period without religion or law), limiting the number of wives to four and preferring and urging monogamy. Thus it might seem strange that Muhammad had a somewhat large number of wives. This is explained by the need to form blood alliances with Arabian tribes by means of marriages and by his desire to "wed and protect" the widow of a famous, but poor, Islamic "martyr." Muhammad did not have any other wives while Khadija was still alive. As he himself said, "If the husband looks with love upon the

Muslim

Muslim *comes from the active participle of the verb* salama, *"to surrender," from the root* slm, *with the sense of "abandonment," meaning submission to the will of God. Various declensions of the root give, among other words,* Muslim *("He who submits");* Islam *(the name of the Islamic religion); and* salaam, *the Muslim salutation, meaning "peace," from the phrase* assalam alaikum, *"peace to you," the response to which is* alaikum salam. *The word appears in other languages: Shalom, Solomon, and Salome.*

wife, and the wife looks with love upon the husband, God looks with love on both." Over the centuries, this Hadith has been seen as an incentive to monogamy. The verse of the Koran (4:3) that limits the number of wives to four, with preference to monogamy, runs: *If you are apprehensive that you shall not deal fairly with orphans, then, of other women who seem good in your eyes, marry but two, or three, or four; and if you still fear that you shall not act equitably, then one only.* Clearly, the concern is the care for orphans that have been adopted and those cases in which a single woman was not enough to raise them. The fact remains that, far from being a kind of licentiousness, as some have suggested, this put a limit on polygamy, which was not abolished by either the Old or New Testament, such that Luther, Bucer, Melanchthon, and others held it permissible in Christianity, beginning with Matthew 25:1–12. Furthermore, during the period of Charlemagne, even Christian priests practiced polygamy, nor are there even today restrictions on it among Zoroastrians, Hindus, and other peoples. Muhammad's household cannot have been completely restful, since several of his wives had very strong characters, and Islam had given them a freedom that they had not originally had. The Prophet offered them the chance to depart with a large dowry, but they refused, as can be read in the Koran (33:28): *If ye desire this present life and its braveries, come then, I will provide for you, and dismiss you with an honorable dismissal.*

ونحل الصفا والحبلا والله والنبي بالله انها لفعلت بالله فاضاعت سقم من
فعشه ملازما ماداني قدمت بالرفق درهما وقطعه وقلت لها ارغبن قي المتوفى لم لم
وارسلن الي الدرهم فوجه الي الثمن المقعد وان ابنا لان ترجح منها المقطعه واشرطن

قالت الي استخلاص البدر النم والابلج الهمر وقالت فتح جدالك ينج جدالك بالك فانخط
طلع الشيخ ولدته والشغر وابح بردته فقالت ان الشيخ من اهلن زوج وهو النبي وتن

Left: Arabian horsemen celebrate a victory, miniature by Yahia al-Wasiti for the *Maqamat* of al-Hariri, 1273, National Library, Paris.

Opposite top: Angel of Victory, thirteenth-century Seljuk sculpture, Ince Minare madrasa, Konya, Turkey.

Opposite bottom: Site of the battle of Uhud.

THE DEFEAT AT UHUD

Muhammad now made his first alliances with Bedouin tribes (who remained faithless; the Koran relates how the Prophet always feared their betrayals) and ordered small attacks made on Meccan caravans. The Quraysh soon decided to put an end to this and assembled an army of three thousand men, put it under the command of Abu Sufyan, and had it follow one of their valuable caravans. When the Muslims attacked at Uhud, the Quraysh, alerted to this raid by the Banu Nadir, a Jewish tribe of Mecca, attacked. The outcome was long uncertain, but just as it seemed to turn in favor of the Muslims, the archers Muhammad had placed to protect his flanks abandoned their posts to chase the fleeing caravan. At the same time, word spread that the Prophet was dead; the Quraysh Khalid ibn al-Walid profited from the situation and soon had the upper hand.

The battle became a rout, and among the dead Muslims was Hamza, an uncle of Muhammad. The Meccans did not profit from this victory,

and the defeated took refuge at Medina without excessive losses. The Koran (3:140–144 and 165–171) admonishes those who fled the field and the hypocrites who had not participated in the war or had not obeyed Muhammad. To mitigate the defeat, Muhammad besieged the Jewish tribe of the Banu Nadir. Holed up in their well-fortified houses, they held out for several weeks; then, defeated, they

emigrated, some moving to Khaybar, others to the north.

On this subject the Koran (59:2) says: *He it is who caused the unbelievers among the people of the book to quit their homes and join those who had emigrated previously. Ye did not think that they would quit them; and they on their part thought that their fortresses would protect them against God . . . But Allah came upon them whence they looked not for him and cast such fear into their hearts that by their own hands as well as by the hands of the victorious believers they demolished their houses. Profit by this example, ye who are men of insight!*

The next year (AH 5, or 626–27), a coalition of Banu Qurayza Jews of Medina, Quraysh, and Bedouin warrior tribes (including the Kinana, Ghatafan, Fazara, Murra, Sulaym, Asad, and Ashja) formed an army of about 10,000 men; they could also count on assistance from Medina itself, from part of the *munafiqun*: "hypocrites." Muhammad managed to arm about 3,000 Muslims and had a ditch (*khandaq*) dug in those areas around the city that were poorly protected— a new strategy for that time and place. The idea may have been suggested to him by a freed Persian slave who had converted to Islam: Salman Pak, called al-Farisi (the Persian).

The Muslims did not confront the enemy and

limited themselves to withstanding the siege. Eventually a cold wind, the lack of food, and internal dissension broke the will of the besiegers, who left the field. This was certainly one of the most important moments in the early history of Islam, and the Koran (33:9–25) has much to say about it.

Once the besiegers left, Muhammad declared war on the last Jewish tribe, the Banu Qurayza, who had

comest nigh unto a city to fight against it, then proclaim peace unto it. And it shall be, if it make thee answer of peace, and open unto thee, then it shall be, that all the people that is found therein shall be tributaries unto thee, and they shall serve thee. And if it will make no peace with thee, but will make war against thee, then thou shalt besiege it: And when the Lord thy God hath delivered it unto thine hands,

Opposite top: Ingenuous miniature commemorating the defeat at Uhud.
Opposite bottom: Two pages from the *Book of Sciences* by Ya'qub ben

Khazzam, fourteenth century, Academy of Sciences, St. Petersburg.
Above: One of the fortified houses of the Banu Qurayza on the outskirts of Medina.

thou shalt smite every male thereof with the edge of the sword; but the women, and the little ones, and the cattle, and all that is in the city, even all the spoil thereof, shalt thou take unto thyself; and thou shalt eat the spoil of thine enemies." And the Koran (33:26) states: *And he caused those of the people of the book who had aided the confederates to come down out of their fortresses, and cast dismay into their hearts: some ye slew, others ye took prisoner.*

instigated the coalition, paid part of its expenses, and sought to spread discord among the Muslims of Medina. After a siege of twenty-five days, the Banu Quaryza were forced to surrender. Muhammad had them choose their judge; they chose Sa'd, son of Mu'adh of the Aws. He did not apply Islamic law but rather Jewish (Deuteronomy 20:10–17): "When thou

Muhammad instructed that more trenches be dug; all the Jewish men were then led out in groups and beheaded.

Left: On the orders of the Prophet Muhammad, Ali chops down a tree worshipped by the inhabitants of Mecca.

Bottom: Gabriel shows Ali's valor to the Prophet, miniature from Shiraz, ca. 1480, Museum of Decorative Arts, Teheran.

Opposite: The construction of the first mosque in Medina (the construction of the "rival mosque" was very similar), in an eighteenth-century Turkish miniature, Topkapi Palace Library, Istanbul.

THE TRAGEDY OF AISHA

Safe in Medina, the Prophet undertook a long series of expeditions to the north, including one against the Banu Lihyan, with whom he made an accord, and one against the Banu al-Mustaliq, in the course of which an event occurred that was full of future consequences. On their way home, the Muslims camped in the desert and the fifteenth wife of the Prophet, Aisha, daughter of Abu Bakr, left the camp without telling anyone to look for a pearl necklace she had recently lost. In her absence the men struck camp and departed, believing that little Aisha was in her palanquin. When she returned to the site of the camp, she stayed there, believing they would return for her. She spent the night there. The next morning a young man passed by, Sufian, son of Unattil. He saw her and took her on his camel to Medina.

For the enemies of Muhammad, this was a golden opportunity for a campaign of slander in

which the girl, completely unaware of what was happening, was accused of having committed adultery. The campaign was organized by Ibn Ubayy, who would have become the leader of Medina had Muhammad not arrived. As a result of this, the Prophet later treated his young wife with a certain coldness, such that she chose to return to her mother's home. Ali, the Prophet's cousin and son-in-law, suggested that he repudiate Aisha. So it was that the verses that completely exonerate Aisha descended (24:11–20), establishing the legal norms in regard to accusations of adultery (24:4–5).

The event was to have unfortunate effects on Islam. Aisha never forgave Ali for his suggestion and from then on nourished an implacable hatred of him that ended, after Muhammad's death, in a series of bloody acts: the assassination of the third caliph, Uthman, in 656; the battle against Ali's followers on December 9, 656, called the Battle of the Camel because Aisha watched it from her camel; and the assassination of Ali in 661, which led to the scission of the Muslims into Sunni and Shiite.

All of which reveals the climate of concealed hostility in which Muhammad was forced to operate even when among his own followers. Other events confirm this. Nasr, son of Harith, fled with several apostates; one of the Prophet's secretaries, Abd-Allah, son of Sa'd, a "protégé" of Uthman, disturbed Muhammad with his coarseness and then fled to Mecca, where he began a violent campaign slandering the Muslims, claiming he himself would be able to compose a Koran. He was later forgiven and became a capable general and statesman. The most serious event occurred when Muhammad found himself busy in the victorious campaign of Tabuk (AH 9: 630). At the instigation of the monk Abu Amir (who had already tried to make the Prophet fall into a hole covered with branches), a "rival mosque" was created at

Medina. Informed of this while at Awan during his return, the Prophet sent a group of the faithful to destroy it. As the Koran (9:107) says: *There are some who have built a mosque for mischief and for infidelity, and to disunite the faithful, and in expectation of him who, in time past, warred against God and his apostle. They will surely swear, "Our aim was only good": but God is witness that they are liars.*

In March 628 (Dhu al-Qada, AH 6), Muhammad set off from Medina with a group of the faithful, intending to make a small pilgrimage (*umra*) to Mecca. They camped at Hudaybiyya and sent Uthman off to the Quraysh with the request for access to the city. When Uthman was late returning, the companions feared he had been killed. The Prophet had them stand beneath a tree and swear allegiance to him, but just then Uthman returned with a response: the Quraysh refused to let the group enter the Holy City at that time, but agreed that they could make the umra the next year in exchange for ten years of peace—ten years during which the Muslims would not attack the Quraysh caravans. Muhammad accepted and performed the sacrifices related to the pilgrimage there in Hudaybiyya, although his companions pressed for war. Muhammad's diplomatic astuteness here achieved its highest moment, making this an important moment for understanding Muhammad's stature, his strength of spirit and character. In the face of the stubbornness of the Meccans and the fanatical impatience of many of his companions, who wanted to attack the Quraysh, he chose instead diplomacy and patience. He returned to Medina; later events would prove he had been fully in the right.

He conquered, in May 628, the rich Jewish oasis of Khaybar, then Wadi al-Qura, where he instituted the "capitation" (*jizya*): a tax to be paid by those of other religions who wished to reside within Muslim territory without embracing Islam. This tax, which reached its most complete form during the Abbasid period, consisted of a fixed sum to be paid at the beginning of every lunar year by every adult free male, thus excluding the old, women, invalids, slaves, mendicants, the ill, and the mentally deranged. Foreigners staying in an Islamic country for less than a year were exempted, as were people from borderlands enlisted in military expeditions, even if they were not Muslim. Like the Muslim *zakat*, this tax was used to pay pensions and perform charitable and pious works.

Left: The Prophet heals a wounded fawn, eighteenth-century Turkish miniature, Topkapi Palace Library, Istanbul.

Opposite top: One of the locks that sealed the door of the Ka'ba in Mecca, damascened iron, fifteenth century.

Opposite bottom: Casting stones at the pillar symbolic of Satan during the great pilgrimage to Mecca.

The Peaceful Conquest of Mecca

On March 7, 629 (AH 7), Muhammad made the umra, following the agreement made with the Quraysh the preceding year. With 2,000 followers he entered the city, which the Meccans had left nearly deserted for three days. Bilal ibn Rabah, the black slave who was Islam's first muezzin, climbed to the roof of the Ka'ba and called the faithful to prayer. Muhammad spoke with several leading men

to Islam could prove useful, and among the new allies was the important tribe of the Sulaym.

In Mecca, the party opposed to the Prophet was getting the upper hand but just then committed an error, giving support to the Bakr clan against the clan of the Khuza'a, allies of Muhammad. According to the customs of the time, this act was the equivalent of breaking the treaty of Hudaybiyya. In the month of Ramadan, AH 8 (December 629–January 630), Muhammad set off from Medina with 10,000

and converted them to his religion. Among these were the general Amr ibn al'As and most of all Khalid ibn al-Walid, later to be one of the most valiant Islamic conquerors. Muhammad then married the sister-in-law of Abbas and requested permission to prolong his stay so as to celebrate the nuptials, but this the Quraysh did not permit.

On his return to Medina, the Prophet prepared an expedition against the Byzantines of Jordan; but at Mu'ta, to the south of Kerak, the Muslims suffered a bloody defeat. Among the dead were Ja'far ibn Abi Talib and Muhammad's adopted son, Zayd ibn Haritha. Theophanes the Confessor (758–818) refers to this battle in his *Chronographia*, which is the first historical mention of Muslims outside the Arabian Peninsula. Despite its outcome, this expedition made many Arab tribes realize that adhesion

faithful—Muhajirun, Aansar, and Bedouins—and headed toward Mecca with the avowed purpose of carrying out the pilgrimage, nothing more. But the Meccans feared the worst: by then isolated and powerless, they thought it best to reach an agreement

with Muhammad. They sent Abu Sufyan to draw up a formal agreement with him. In substance, this meant victory without delivering a blow. When he reached the Ka'ba, Muhammad found an assembly of Quraysh leaders. He spoke to them, promising no mistreatment, no vendettas, and a general amnesty with only a few exceptions. Most of all he offered confirmation of the ranks and roles of the leading families as custodians of the Holy City, which Mecca was to continue to be with Islam, while the Prophet would remain in the political capital, Medina. Following this the idols were overturned.

A new danger now appeared. The Hawazin Bedouin tribes of central Arabia (Banu Sa'd, Banu Bakr, Banu Hilal, Banu Sulayman), the strongest and most dangerous Bedouin group near the Holy City, always hostile to the Quraysh even if sporadically allied with them, decided to march against Medina and Muhammad. The Prophet organized his troops; the leader of

The Ka'ba during the great pilgrimage to the holy city of Mecca, eighty years ago (*above*) and today (*below*).

Opposite: The Sassanid emperor Yazdagird reading a letter from the Prophet, Iranian miniature, National Library, Paris.

Mecca, Abu Sufyan, provided weapons. On January 26, 630, the Muslim army, with twelve to sixteen thousand men, marched toward the valley of Hunayn. The battle took place four days later. Led by Malik, son of Auf, the Bedouins had the upper hand in the beginning, as some of the Prophet's confederates abandoned the field. In response Muhammad yelled, "O Ansar, who helped the Prophet! O you who took the oath of allegiance under the tree at Hudaybiyya! Where are you going? The Prophet is here!" The Muslims who had been breaking ranks returned, and with the call *"Labbayka!"* ("Here I am!") were victorious. The spoils included 24,000 camels and rams, along with many prisoners. At that point the Hawazin converted en masse to Islam and the prisoners were set free.

The Prophet then laid siege to the fortified city of Ta'if, a long siege that proved fruitless. Only a year later, when Muhammad won the great victory of Tabuk with about 30,000 men, did the city decide to accept Islam. The Prophet spent about ten days at Tabuk, during which he accepted the submission of many northern oases and cities, both Christian and Jewish, including the maritime city of Makna, that of Adhruh, and Ayla, with its Christian prince, Yuhanna. Meanwhile, General Khalid conquered the stronghold of Dumat al-Jandal, an oasis on the Medina–Damascus route that two previous Muslim expeditions had failed to take.

Muhammad had succeeded in performing the "miracle" no one had dared to dream possible. Until then, the warlike tribes of Arabia had fought one another in endless feuds and wars, events sung about in poems that only fed the bellicose spirits. Now an *umma* was taking form, a brotherhood of all the Muslim peoples in which the only distinction would be between good and bad faithful. Other tribes of the center, south, and north of the peninsula soon joined Islam, among them the Amir ibn Sa'sa'a, frac-

tions of the great Tamim tribe, of the Asad, and farther to the north the Bakr and Taghlib. Some regions under the influence of Iran, such as Bahrain and Oman, and several principalities of southern Arabia also embraced the religion. The alliance and the unity of the Arab peoples grew stronger daily, while the Koran taught respect for foreigners, for those who were different, for the property of others, a respect the Arabs had never before known.

DEATH OF THE PROPHET

In AH 9 (630–31), the Christian population of Najran sent a delegation to Muhammad composed of about sixty learned men led by a bishop named Abu Harita. The Prophet permitted them to celebrate Mass in his mosque, after which he debated with them on the nature of Christ. The delegation held that Islam's position was the same as that of the archimandrite in Constantinople, Eutyches (ca. 378–454), meaning Monophysitic, a doctrine rejected by the Council of Chalcedon in 451.

Since both sides were not budging from their positions, Muhammad proposed an ordeal (*muba-hala*), as related in the Koran (3:61): *After the knowledge which hath come unto thee* [the history of

Below: The Prophet's last sermon in Medina, eighteenth-century Turkish miniature, Topkapi Palace Library, Istanbul.

Above: The death of the Prophet.

Opposite: The tomb of the Prophet at Medina, sixteenth-century Iraqi miniature.

Jesus, from when Mary withdrew in solitude to his birth and mission, is narrated in the preceding verses, 35–60], *come, let us summon our sons and your sons, and our wives and your wives, and ourselves and yourselves. Then will we invoke and lay the curse of God on those who lie.*

This ordeal, in which the contenders reciprocally invoked divine curses and death on those who made false affirmations, was a typical custom of the period. Muhammad went to the site chosen for the ordeal, holding his nephews Hasan and Husain by the hand; he was followed by his daughter Fatima and son-in-law Ali. He wore a tunic of black goatskin trimmed in silk. When the Christians arrived on the site, they chose instead to propose to the Prophet the payment of a per-person tax in exchange for the free exercise of their religion and the respect of their persons. They thus became the first *Dhimmi*, non-Muslims that Islam permitted in its territory (such permission being in keeping with *Shari'a*, Islamic law) and granted freedom of wor-

ship in exchange for payment of an annual tax. This was also in accord with the Koran (2:62, 5:69, and 22:17): *Lo! Those who believe and those who are Jews and the Sabaeans and the Christians and whosoever believeth in Allah and the last day and doeth which is right shall have their reward with their Lord: fear shall not come upon them, neither shall they be grieved.*

At the same time, however, a movement of rebellion was taking shape among the new Muslims because the new state was beginning to demand payment of taxes from everyone, something which the clans found unacceptable. After all the many centuries of living in tribal anarchy, they considered themselves completely independent. The closest Arabic term for tax, *jizya*, is derived from the same root as "punishment" and its masculine form means "ruin, punishment"; thus, the preferred term came to be *zakat* (official charity, understood as a community's religious duty). Medina itself, now considerably enriched, rebuked the Prophet, claiming he

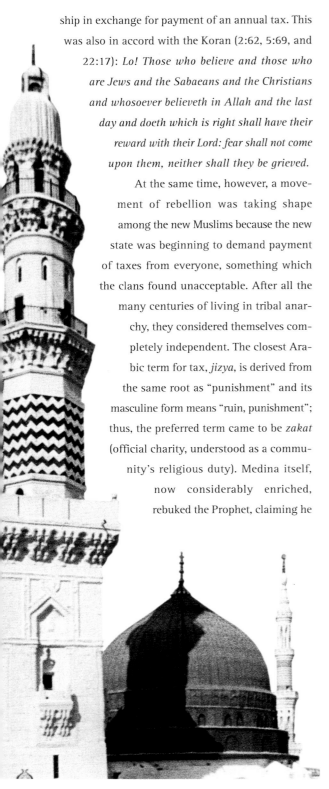

favored the Quraysh in the division of spoils, and this even though Muhammad had not made Mecca the capital of his new state.

In the month of Dhu al-Hijja in AH 10 (February/March 632) Muhammad, in the company of 140,000 Muslims, made his last pilgrimage to Mecca. Si Hamza Boubakeur writes: "In his sermon he repeated the call to abandon oneself to the single God and emphasized respect for the rights of women, for human brotherhood, for the equality of all human beings, which differ only in terms of their merits, their virtue, their faith; he condemned every form of racism, usury, misappropriation. The Koran was proclaimed as an inviolable and imperishable testament, the testimony of divine mercy on all human beings." Muhammad then recited Sura 5:3: *This day have I perfected your religion for you and have filled up the measure of my favors upon you; and it is my pleasure that Islam be your religion;*

but whoso without willful leanings to wrong shall be forced by hunger to transgress, to him, verily, will God be indulgent, merciful. Then Sura 110 descended, its three verses a clear allusion to his imminent death: *When the help of God and the victory arrive, and thou seest men entering the religion*

of God by troops; then utter the praise of thy Lord, implore his pardon; for he loveth to turn in mercy.

Muhammad's mission had been completed. He returned to Medina, to his home, and during the early hours of the afternoon of the thirteenth day of Rabi in AH 11 (June 8, 632), he died, whispering words that were remembered by his daughter Fatima: "For me the affliction is finished. O Allah, with the supreme communion." Umar wanted to keep his death a secret, but Abu Bakr went out to the faithful at prayer and spoke to them, beginning with these words from the Koran (3:144–45): *Muhammad is no more than an apostle; other apostles have already passed away before him: if he die, therefore, or be slain, will ye turn upon your heels? But he who turneth on his heels shall not injure God at all. And God will certainly reward the thankful. No one can die except by God's permission, according to the book that fixeth the term of life.*

The Five Pillars of Islam
(arkan al-Din)

There are five holy prescriptions (*fara'idh*) in Islam.

1. The profession of faith (*Shahada*). The believer expresses his faith in the oneness of God by repeating the affirmation *la ilaha illa Allah, Muhammad rasulu Allah:* "There is no God but God, and Muhammad is the messenger of God." The person who speaks this affirmation before two Muslim witnesses becomes him- or herself a Muslim.

2. The canonical prayers (*salat*, plural *salawat*). There are five of these: between dawn and daybreak (*subh*); when the sun passes the zenith (*dhuhr*); in the late afternoon (*asr*); at sunset (*maghrib*); at the onset of night (*isha*). They are preceded by ritual ablutions if needed and are performed in an open place without images, facing the Ka'ba (*qibla*).

3. The payment of obligatory charity (*zakat*). This is a small annual payment that is used to maintain the mosque and see to the needs of the poor, children, widows, and orphans. Needy non-Muslims can also make use of it.

Below: Interior of the mosque of Eyub, Turkey.

PRAYER IN ISLAM

1. The ablution (*wudu*) before prayer. There are three types of ablution: the greater (*ghusl*), the lesser (*wudu asghar*), and the dry (*tayammum*).

4. The believer kneels with hands on knees, then prostrates himself and speaks the praise of God, begging his forgiveness.

2. After expressing the intention to pray, the faithful raises his hands and proclaims, "Allahu akbar," and then the *iqama*.

5. Kneeling, the faithful speaks appropriate formulas. This completes the first *rak'a* (cycle of ritual actions and phrases). The believer begins from the beginning, and when he returns to this position speaks specific formulas.

3. The believer speaks the *Fatiha* followed by at least five verses of the Koran or one entire sura. At the beginning of every movement he says, "Allahu akbar."

6. The believer turns his head to right, saying, "Al Salam alaykum wa Rahmat al-Lah," then he turns to the left. Prayer is finished. Each of the five canonical prayers has its number of appropriate *rak'a*.

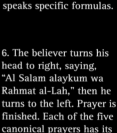

4. The fast during the month of Ramadan (*siyam*). From dawn to dusk the faithful abstains from food, water, tobacco, perfumes, and sexual relations. Prepubescent children, the elderly, and the mentally ill are excused. Pregnant and nursing women, the ill, and travelers can postpone the fast to a more convenient time. Taking medicine is allowed.

5. The pilgrimage to Mecca (*hajj*). At least once in his life, every Muslim must make the pilgrimage to Mecca if he is adult, mentally fit, physically capable, and free to do so. The pilgrimage is not to be undertaken by those who cannot afford it or for whom the expense would constitute a damage to the family, nor should it be undertaken if doing so requires traveling across territory made dangerous, as by war or disease. The rite of the pilgrimage takes place in the first ten days of the month of Dhu al-Hijja and includes special clothing (*ihram*), the arrival circumambulation of the Ka'ba seven times (*tawaf*), seven runs between the hills of Safa and Marwa (*sa'y*), a visit to Arafat (*waqfa*), the collection of forty-nine stones at Muzdalifa, casting stones (*ramy*) several times at the pillar of Satan, and the sacrifice of an animal at Mina (*nahr*). There is finally the farewell circumambulation of the Ka'ba (*tawaf al-Wada*). Some schools accept the "pilgrimage by proxy," but others oppose it.

The Essence of Islam

The servants of the God of Mercy are they who walk upon the earth softly; and when the ignorant address them, they reply, "Peace!" They commit no obscene acts; They do not slay whom God hath forbidden to be slain. They do not bear witness to what is false, and when they pass by frivolous sport, they pass on with dignity; And when the verses of God are recited they are not deaf (Koran 25:63–76).

The Four "Rightly Guided" Caliphs

The Prophet Muhammad seems to have intended to transmit his temporal powers (the "elective caliphate") to his cousin and son-in-law Ali, son of Abi Talib. As a result of intrigues and opposition from Abu Sufyan; Umar, son of Khattab; and the Prophet's young widow, Aisha, an assembly of Ansar and Muhajirun chose Abu Bakr as their new leader. Thus began what came to be called "the struggle with the family of the Prophet." Abu Bakr ruled until 634, struggling against every attempt at apostasy (*ridda*). On the urging of Umar, who had become his direct adviser, he began the compilation of the Koran, for the first time collecting the vari-ous pronouncements of the Prophet that had been taken down by the Prophet's many secretaries and enlisting the cooperation of those who had memorized the entire sacred text. Abu Bakr was succeeded by Umar. A skilled organizer, Umar instituted an independent magistrate and carried on the conquest of surrounding territories. He was also responsible for the creation of the postal service and the pension plan for soldiers, for legislation for non-Muslims, and the institution of the Muslim year beginning with Muhammad's emigration to Medina (hegira). In 640 he established the principle of the elective caliphate and the title of "commander of the believers" (*amir al-Mum'inin*). He was responsible for the victory over the Sassanids at Kadisiya (637)—an important victory that opened central Asia to Islam—and the conquest of Egypt (641). He was assassinated by opponents in 644 and buried at Medina beside the tomb of Muhammad.

Umar was succeeded by Uthman ibn Affan, who in time was accused of overly favoring the interests of his clan. For example, he gave governorships to his half-brother Walid and to his foster brother Abdallah ibn Sa'd, already proscribed by Muhammad; a verse against him in the Koran (6:93) had "descended" on the Prophet. During this period the

Left: Abu Bakr elected legitimate successor of the Prophet, eighteenth-century Turkish miniature.

Above and opposite bottom: The names of the four "rightly guided" caliphs, on twentieth-century ceramics in a mosque in Milan, Italy.

Opposite top: The name of Abu Bakr in the Hagia Sophia, Istanbul.

naval victory over the Byzantines took place (652), as well as the conquests of Cyprus (649) and much of North Africa (648).

In 655, Uthman was assassinated by Muhammad, son of Abu Bakr, and the struggle with the family of Muhammad reached a resolution with the nomination to caliph of Ali, who moved the capital from Medina to Kufa. His rule was not without disputes. Aisha, Muhammad's widow, opposed him and fought his army in the Battle of the Camel (656), which took place near Basra and led to the *fitna* (division of the Islamic community). Uthman's nephew Muawiya, of the Banu Umayya tribe, also opposed him and fought his army in the battle of Siffin (657), which led to Kharijism (one of the two great historical divisions of Islam, the other being Shiism). Ali was assassinated at Kufa in 661 by a Kharijite separatist, and his son, Hasan, was elected caliph; but his rival Muawiya had him poisoned and, abusing the elective process, proclaimed himself king, founding the Umayyad caliphate and moving the capital from Kufa to Damascus. Thus the Banu Umayya—a clan of great Meccan caravan merchants always hostile to the Prophet who had converted only at the last moment—took power. Si Hamza Boubakeur wrote: "The assassination at Kufa, in the middle of Ramadan of the year 41 [January 661] of the legitimate caliph, the undisputed hero of Islam ... the passage of power to a family that had originally been ferociously hostile to Islam and to the Prophet, the Banu Umayya,

the movement of the political capital of Islam to Damascus ... did not fail to disturb the feelings and devotion of the first generation of Muslims. The Islam of the proletariat was deprived of power by the very bankers that had first violently opposed it and whose religious fervor was somewhat tepid. That disgusted those who had helped win its triumph over idolatry. Despite the fundamentally egalitarian and antiracist spirit of Islam, the Arabs wanted to set the style and benefit from racial and political power over the other Muslim peoples."

The "sect" (*Shi'a, Shi'ite, Shiite*), upholders of the legitimacy of the Alid family, and the so-called Medina companions of Muhammad aligned against the Umayyads, who included the Meccans. The Shiites were defeated several times, and in the slaughter at Karbala (October 10, 680), Husein, Ali's second son, much

Left: Interior of the Hagia Sophia, Istanbul, with the tondo bearing the name of the last "rightly guided" caliph, Ali; the calligraphy is by Izzet Efendi (1756–1849).

Opposite top: The mosque of Turfan (1777, Chinese Turkestan) with the high minaret of Sultan Imin covered in brick decoration emblematic of five religions of China.

Opposite bottom: The expansion of Islam up to the fall of the Umayyad dynasty in 750.

loved by Muhammad, was betrayed and murdered. The Shiite revolt was finally put down in 698, but the "sect of Ali" transformed into a religious movement with mysterious "adventist" traits, becoming the largest division (having a political rather than a doctrinal character, it is not truly a schism) in Islam. Boubakeur wrote: "The division caused by the Umayyads, the discredit of Islamic values, the decay of customs, the favoritism and corruption, the transformation of the elective caliphate into dynastic power as a result of pressures of all kinds and through

the attraction of money inevitably had profound repercussions on the consciences of the pious, beginning with disgust and indignation at the turn of events ... At the beginning of the dynasty of the usurpers the centers of mysticism multiplied at Kufa, Basra, Medina, Mecca, in Yemen, in Khorasan, and came to number a great many of pro-Alid mystics, intransigents, and those faithful to the memory of the Prophet. All of these were marked by eloquence, by criticism of customs, by the habit of making a spiritual withdrawal in mosques."

THE EARLY SPREAD OF ISLAM

During this period, the Moors, a nomadic people primarily from northwest Africa, conquered Spain in 711 and invaded France in 732, being turned back at Poitiers. In Spain, nine provinces of Andalusia were taken by Iranian troops in 742; thus one can speak of an Islamic-Spanish civilization, but not of an Arab-Spanish one. To the east, by 713, Islamic expansion had reached the Indus River delta. This century of the Umayyads was dominated by the Arabs and their mentality, a reality that the conquered peoples—who had superior cultures, civilizations, artistic tastes, and histories—poorly supported. Fully 50,000 Arab families moved to Khorasan in 665, but by 733 their number was down to 15,000, and one hundred years later they had been forced to relocate toward the Arabian Peninsula.

In 750 Abu Abbas, descendant of Muhammad's uncle, joined the Shiite faction and destroyed the Umayyad dynasty, founding that of the Abbasids

and moving the capital to Baghdad, near Ctesiphon, former capital of the Sassanian Empire. Baghdad thus came to be symbolic of the gradual Iranization and Turkification of the vast Islamic world, which then extended to the borders of China and the Indus River, to Samarkand, to the Atlantic, and in Spain up to the Pyrenees. Soon enough, the Turkish element, which came from central Asia—and had originally been introduced as a special military unit

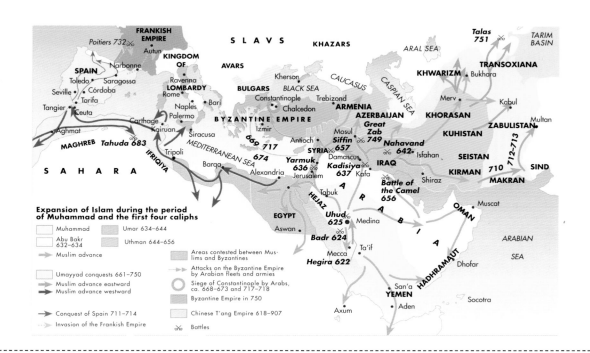

Expansion of Islam during the period of Muhammad and the first four caliphs

- Muhammad
- Abu Bakr 632–634
- Umar 634–644
- Uthman 644–656
- Muslim advance
- Umayyad conquests 661–750
- Muslim advance eastward
- Muslim advance westward
- Conquest of Spain 711–714
- Invasion of the Frankish Empire
- Areas contested between Muslims and Byzantines
- Attacks on the Byzantine Empire by Arabian fleets and armies
- Siege of Constantinople by Arabs, ca. 668–673 and 717–718
- Byzantine Empire in 750
- Chinese T'ang Empire 618–907
- Battles

Arabian period, which like the paleo-Christian, Armenian, and Byzantine had been an outgrowth of the late classical, came to an end, replaced by a civilization, culture, and arts that were fundamentally Islamic. This civilization was composed of contributions from Iranians, Turks, Afghans, Indians, Egyptians, North Africans, and Andalusians. The Turks in particular succeeded in amalgamating these various trends and did so thanks to three factors: political power (with the conquest of India and Iran, and then of Anatolia and the Balkans, two territories that the Arabs had sought in vain to occupy);

for defense of the court—got the upper hand and in 836 founded a new, colossal capital: Samarra. The rule of Egypt was entrusted to the Turk Ibn Tulun (868); the Iranian provinces became autonomous first under Tahir (820), then Mazayr (839–40); finally the Iranian dynasty of the Buwayhids took power (945) and formed a vast empire that was later conquered by the Seljuk Turks (1050), who entered Baghdad led by Toghril Beg in 1055.

So it was that Islam became universal. The

Napoleon Bonaparte

"Muhammad was a prince; he gathered his compatriots around himself and in a few years they conquered half the world. In fifteen years they tore more souls from false gods, knocked over more idols, and destroyed more pagan temples than did the followers of Moses and Jesus Christ in fifteen centuries. Muhammad was a great man."

Napoleon Bonaparte (1769–1821),
Campagne d'Égypte et de Syrie

artistic depth (achieving a great synthesis of the abstract art of the nomads of the steppe of central Asia with the late classical, sedentary, and figurative styles); and commercial talent (heirs to the Silk Route, they ran the great Europe-Asia-Africa caravan routes, with all the consequent exchanges of ideas and knowledge).

All these non-Arabic peoples (the North Africans, as indicated earlier, should be considered at most to be Arabic-speaking peoples) applied their particular traditions to the Islamic religion, giving a powerful impulse to what can be called its mystical side, Sufism. The Arab language—adopted as the administrative language by the caliph Abd al-Malik (685–705)—was still used as the language of religion and sciences, much as Latin was used in Europe. The Persian language took its place beside it, most of all after the great poet Firdausi (935–1020) used it for his *Shahnama* (*Book of Kings*), an epic exaltation of the refined Iranian tradition (which he wrote for Mahmud of Ghazni, Turkish king of Afghanistan). In the larger and more enlightened Islamic Empire of the Ottomans—who conquered Constantinople in 1453—Turkish came into use as the administrative language. The Arabian contingents of the conquest were driven back to their places of origin, with the exception of small groups that were fully assimilated, and then the Arabian Peninsula fell back into its age-old *jahiliyya*.

Muslims Conquering the World

Having followed the succession of the first four caliphs, along with some of the evolution of the science of religion that came to form the structure—what might be called the bureaucracy—of the Islamic religion, we can now rapidly review Islam's territorial expansion, its worldly aspect, a matter with which even the most sublime concept must come to terms, since it involves human beings.

Muawiya, the first Umayyad caliph, introduced the dynastic principle to Islam, doing away with the election of the religious and political leader, which is suggested by the Koran itself (42:38): *They who hearken to their Lord, and observe prayer, and whose affairs are guided by mutual counsel.* The Syrians learned Arabic, which became their official language, and the Syrian Umayyad dynasty (661–750) conquered North Africa (697–707) and founded Kairouan, or Al Qayrawan (670). The Moors conquered Spain (712) and invaded Merovingian France until defeated at Poitiers (732). To the east, Muslims

Left: The emperor Malik Shah.
Below: The castle in Syria begun by Harun al-Rashid and finished by Saladin.
Bottom: The walls of Rabat, Morocco.

Opposite top: The great mosque of the Umayyads in Damascus, Syria.
Opposite center: Corner of the Gulistan Palace in Teheran.
Opposite bottom: Portrait of the Turkish-Afghan prince of Hetimandel, India, seventeenth century.

conquered Iran, Afghanistan (651), Transoxiana (674), and penetrated Chinese Turkestan, Sind, Punjab, and Ude (711). The Muslim Empire thus extended from the Atlantic to the borders of China.

The Umayyads were succeeded by the Abbasids (905–1055), who installed themselves in Iraq and favored the Iranian people. With their capital of Baghdad, they achieved their period of greatest splendor during the reign of Harun ar-Rashid (786–809). Beginning in the ninth century, the growing power of the empire's Turkish mercenaries favored the progressive independence of the more distant provinces. To the west was the independent emirate of Córdoba (756–1031) and the kingdoms of northwest Africa (Maghreb); to the east were the

Iranian kingdoms, out of which came the Samanids (902–999), who supported the birth of an Iranian literature and distinctly Islamic art. The first Turkish Muslim dynasty, the Ghaznavids of Afghanistan (999) conquered northern India, while the second Turkish Muslim dynasty, that of Egypt, led to the states ruled by the Tulunids.

The Umayyad caliphate of Baghdad was thus matched by those of Spain and Egypt, up to the creation of the Fatimid dynasty (903–1171), which made Cairo its capital. A decisive moment came in the early eleventh century with the appearance of the Seljuk Turks. From their origins in Iran they founded a politically, socially, and culturally well-organized empire that rose to be the primary model for all of eastern Islam. At the death of the third Seljuk emperor, Malik Shah, the Seljuk Empire was divided among his three children, leading to the creation of local dynasties in Syria, Mesopotamia, Armenia, and Iran. The most important branch of the Seljuks became that of Anatolia (the sultanate of Rum at Konya, 1092–1327). Meanwhile, North Africa, by then completely independent, saw the succession of the two great dynasties of the Almoravids (1053–1147) and the Almohads (1151–1269).

One of the most tragic events in the history of Islam then occurred (1209): the invasion of the Mongols of Genghis Khan, who conquered the largest empire that has ever existed (from China to Russia), reaching even Jerusalem. The Mongols threatened to continue their invasion into Europe but suffered their first setback at the hands of the Bahrite Mamelukes at Ain Jalu in Syria (1260).

The Mongols of central Asia converted to Islam and formed a great khanate that, at the end of the fourteenth century, was invaded by a Turkic-Mongol from Iran, Tamerlane, whose empire began to collapse after his death. Then began one of the most important periods of Islam in Asia, with the formation of three vast empires: the Mogul in India (1526–1857), the Safavid in Iran (1500–1736), and the Ottoman in Anatolia (1302–1922). The Mogul dynasty was founded by Babur, a descendant of Tamerlane and Genghis Khan; it thus replaced the Delhi Sultanate, which had been India's first Muslim kingdom. Akbar (ruled 1556–1605), one of the greatest Mogul emperors, was one of history's most enlightened sovereigns. The Safavids created a Shiite state in Iran, making their capital at Isfahan one of the most beautiful cities in the world. The Ottoman Empire conquered Constantinople in 1453 (making the city its capital,

The Four Orthodox Schools of Law

Hanafi *Founded by Abu Hanifa al-Nu'man (699–767), an Iraqi who died in prison, having refused the post of supreme judge in Baghdad when he saw he would not be able to act free of political intervention. His school gives importance to free opinion (ra'y), to analogy (qiyas), and to utilitarianism (istihsan), and is relatively simple. The school has an evolutionistic outlook, sees the adaptation of the law to circumstances, and allows liberalism in the resolution of problems of a private order. This school is found primarily in Turkey, central Asia, China, India, and Syria.*

Maliki *Founded by Abu Abd-Allah Malik ibn Anas (712–796) of Medina, for which reason it is also called the Hejaz school. Similar in general to the Hanafi school, it rejects liberal opinion and is strictly orthodox. It is criticized for the opinion that the ends justify the means and for the severity with which it condemns dissidents and sectarians. It is widespread in North Africa, Egypt, Arabia, India, Indonesia, and western Europe.*

Shafi'i *Founded by Abu Abd-Allah ibn Idris al-Shafi'i (767–820), born at Gaza. A student of the imam Malik, he got his training in Baghdad. Thoroughly methodological, the school combines Maliki and Hanafi ideas and has become widespread thanks in large part to the great number of outstanding Shafi'i masters, including the Sufi theologian al-Ghazali (1050–1111) and the traditionalist Nawawi (d. 1277). The school is found in southern Arabia, Syria, Iraq, Pakistan, India, and various parts of Europe and America.*

Hanbali *Founded by Ahmad ibn Muhammad ibn Hanbal (780–855) of Baghdad, a resolute fundamentalist. The school arose during a period of political-religious chaos and was forced to assume an intolerant attitude, with the rejection of innovation, criticism of customs, and rigid doctrine. This backward position came to support an equally backward religious-political movement, Wahabbism. The Hanbali school has slight diffusion in Iraq, Egypt, and Palestine; it is found in the United Arab Emirates and Saudi Arabia between Najad and the Persian Gulf.*

THE KORAN

Muhammad, "Seal of the Prophecy," appears to us in two guises. He is the sociopolitical-economic organizer of his people and of the Islamic religion; he is also the "transmitter" of a divine, immutable word that has remained unchanged since the beginning of humanity, advocated by the patriarch Abraham and repeated by the prophets that have protected it from contamination and corruption. It must be remembered that for centuries millions upon millions of men and women of every ethnic background and social rank have testified that Muhammad is the messenger of God. Day after day, in response to the call to prayer, thousands upon thousands of humans call out the phrase "I testify that there is none worthy of worship except God and that Muhammad is the messenger of God." After which thousands upon thousands of faithful listen to the first sura of the Koran, the *Fatiha*.

Opposite: Portrait of the Mogul emperor Akbar (1556–1605).
Left: Painting on leather of a sovereign, detail of a fourteenth-century ceiling, palace of the Alhambra, Granada.
Below: Large stone reading stand for the Koran, Friday Mosque, Samarkand, Uzbekistan.

Istanbul) and then conquered the Balkans, Hungary, the Russian coast of the Black Sea, Syria, Egypt, Tunisia, Algeria, Iraq, and Mecca. The Ottoman advance was halted at the gates of Vienna, and in the eighteenth century the empire went into decline, in part because of Russian and British intrigues, leading to its final collapse at the end of World War I. The history of modern Turkey began with the creation of the Turkish republic in 1923 by Mestafa Pasha, known as Kemal Atatürk, the strongest, most enlightened, and most liberal state with an Islamic majority.

clusus (Latin for "enclosed garden"), an enclosed space, a "part" of the whole. Many scholars believe instead that it is derived from the Syrian word *surta* ("writing, reading") and attribute it to a verb meaning "to recite," thus giving it the meaning of "a piece of reading."

Specialists of various periods and different religions have studied the totality of the suras and have proposed a chronological order that would begin with the first to be revealed, the sixty-ninth, and would run to the last, Sura 110. The most plausible classification is that of Asyuti (or Suyuti; d. 1505), who also calculated the number of terms (6,616) and the number of letters (323,671) used in the Koran. Each sura has a title (some have more than one, a new one alongside still-accepted antique versions), usually based on a term in one of the sura's verses; along with the title there is an indication of whether the sura was inspired at Mecca or at Medina. With the sole exception of the

All of Islam and all of the words of Islam are contained in this sacred book, the treasure and support of every good Muslim. The Koran has three essential elements: the revelation, the submission to God, and the incentives to correct ethical behavior.

The term *Koran* (or *Qur'an*) is cited about seventy times in the sacred book of Islam. It may be derived from the Syrian word *queryana*, "reading of the scriptures; lesson." Other scholars hold it comes from *qara'a*, "recitation" (a verb used seventeen times in the Koran); or perhaps from *qarana*, "to join or collect." It is also called *al-Kitab*, "the Book, the Writing," a term used 261 times. The Koran is composed of 114 suras; the longest has 287 verses, the shortest only three. *Sura* (plural *suwar*), a term used ten times, probably comes from the root *swr*, the first form of which is *sawara*, "to climb" (e.g., a wall), and the fifth form of which is *tasawwara*, "to be surrounded by a wall; to be enclosed." *Sura* would thus be derived from the verb of the second form, *sawwara*, "to enclose with a wall; to surround with a wall," ideally in reference to a *hortus con-*

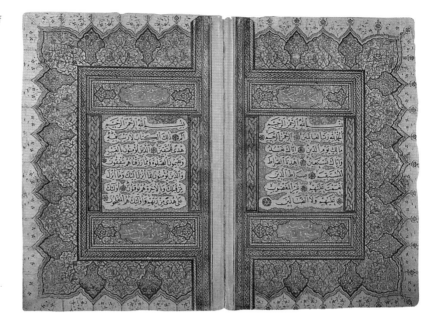

Opposite top: Page of one of the first Korans, on papyrus, eighth/ninth centuries, G. Mandel collection, Milan.

Opposite bottom: The penultimate sura of the Koran reproduced on a twentieth-century ceramic.

Right: Incipit of an Ottoman Koran of the sixteenth century, Topkapi Palace Library, Istanbul.

ninth, each sura is preceded by the phrase *Bismi Allahi al-Rahmani al-Rahimi* ("In the name of Allah, the beneficent, the merciful"). Sometimes the body of a sura contains verses inspired in different places.

The Koran deals with God, the angels, devils, and demons; it deals with the origin and end of the world, resurrection, paradise, and hell. The Koran relates the stories of patriarchs, apostles, and prophets, but states that there are others of which it has not spoken (4:164–65): *Of some prophets we have told thee before: of other prophets we have not told thee, prophets charged to announce and to warn so that men, after those prophets, might have no arguments against God.* The Koran deals with laws and social behavior and rules of life among men and women and between husband and wife, giving women the most protection possible and relating that divorce exists in Islam, that abortion is not prohibited if it is the woman who wants it (for the specific regulations see the great eleventh-century theologian al-Ghazali, in *Ihya Ulumi al-*

Din, II:51–53), that the sexual act is a joy that God has given human beings (Koran 2:223; 187), for which reason contraceptives should be free. There are also calls to study and to increase the sciences, and instructions for fulfilling the Five Pillars of Islam: faith in the oneness of God, daily prayers, charity and taxes (*zakat*), fasting in the month of Ramadan, and the pilgrimage to Mecca.

These Five Pillars are to be carried out only if the believer is an adult, rational, physically fit, and legally free to do so. The first three pillars are obligatory, the last two are conditional and in reality are based on the believer's physical and social state, his environment, and his financial resources. There are other obligations: to not drink alcoholic beverages and to not eat the meat of pigs. Women are not obliged to wear a veil. Although such veils are worn by some peoples, they are not used in a large part of the Islamic world. It is something of a question of uniformity of local habits that often predate the advent of Islam and that can be found in non-Muslim countries.

The Most Important Passages of the Koran

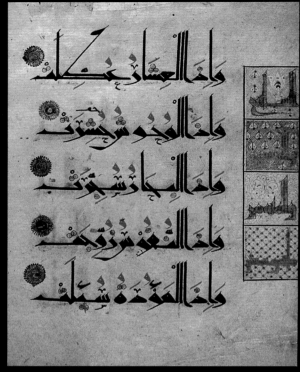

■ The first sura, the *Fatiha:*

In the name of God, the compassionate, the merciful.

Praise be to God, lord of the worlds,

The compassionate, the merciful!

King on the day of reckoning!

Thee only do we worship, and to thee do we cry for help.

Guide us on the straight path, the path of those to whom thou hast been gracious, with whom thou art not angry, and who go not astray.

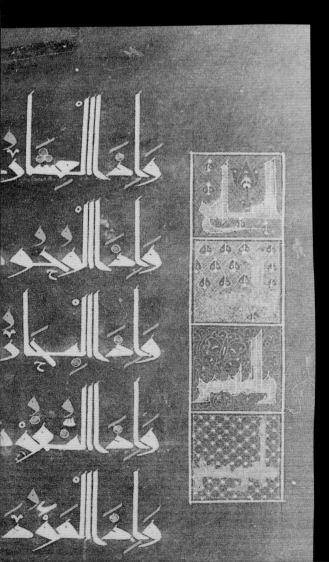

■ The Sura of the Pure Faith (*Alkhlas*), 112:

In the name of God, the compassionate, the merciful.

Say: he is God alone,

God, al-Samad [a difficult term to translate: the eternal, unknowable, absolute, he of whom the world has need while he has need of nothing; the completely different from what we can imagine]

He begetteth not, and he is not begotten.

And there is none like unto him. He is unique.

■ The Verse of the Light (24:35):

God is the light of the heavens and of the earth. His light is like a niche in which is a lamp, the lamp encased in crystal, the crystal like a glistening star. From a blessed tree is it lighted, the olive neither of the East nor of the West, whose oil would well nigh shine out, even though fire touched it not! It is light upon light. God guideth whom he will to his light, and God setteth forth parables to men, for God knoweth all things.

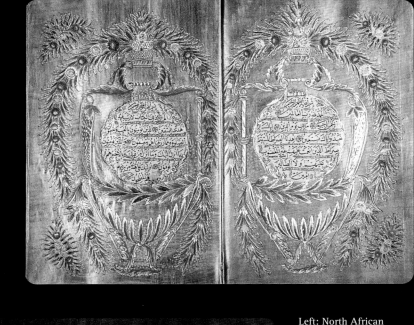

Opposite: Koran in Carmatic kufic, eleventh century, collection of Prince Sadruddin Aga Khan.

Right: North African Koran, seventeenth century, collection of G. Mandel, Milan.

Left: North African Koran, tenth century, collection of Rifat Sheikh al-Ardh, Riyad.

Below: Frontispiece of a Cairo Koran, 1304, British Library, London.

■ The Verse of the Throne (2:255):

God! There is no God but he; the living, the eternal [al-Qayyum: a difficult term to translate: the absolute, he who exists of himself and in whom everything exists].

Nor slumber seizeth him, nor sleep; his is whatsoever is in the heavens and whatsoever is in the earth! Who is he that can intercede with him but by his own permission? He knoweth what hath been before them and what shall be after them; yet nought of his knowledge shall they grasp, save what he willeth. His throne reacheth over the heavens and the earth, and the upholding of both burdeneth him not; he is the high, the great!

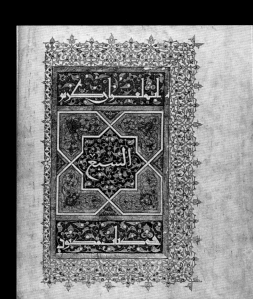

THE "THREE SCIENCES" OF ISLAMIC RELIGION

The Koran does not institute priests and does not seek confession: the Muslim speaks directly to God. Islam has no priests; thus all the various doctors of theology (the *a'imma*—singular *imam*—as well as the mufti and ayatollahs) have carved out a space for themselves in order to acquire power (and they are dishonest if they claim that power in the name of their religion). They came into being by giving explanatory readings and interpretations of the Koran, such interpretations being necessary to Islamic jurisprudence.

Indeed, from the earliest time there has been a "science of the Koran" that has concerned itself with the five rules of its recitation, the eleven types of voice permissible for recitation, and most of all the subdivision of the text into parts so as to better study and memorize it. The text of the Koran was originally handed down by memory, even though the Prophet's secretaries got much of it written down. The Prophet himself recited it all from memory, and before dying (632) had his first secretary, Zayd, son of Thabit, oversee the composition of the first complete version. On Zayd's death this prototype passed to the second caliph, Umar. In 654, the third caliph, Uthman, entrusted the prototype to a commission of experts (who arranged it not in the chronological order of the suras but, beginning with the second sura, more or less according to length). He also had copies made and sent to the capital cities of the various Muslim provinces. These copies had been composed without the use of short vowels (as is typical of Hebrew and Arabic writing); the fully vocalized and therefore definitive version dates to the early tenth century. A group of theologians—at least eleven—then arose to study the variations among editions

Above: The term *alim* ("the wise one, he who has studied the three sciences") on a twentieth-century ceramic.

Left: The Mogul emperor Akbar speaking with wise men of various religions.

Opposite top: Bukhari discusses his selection of Hadith.

Opposite center: The rector of Al-Azhar in Cairo in a painting by Arthur Ferrais (1856–1918), private collection, London.

Opposite bottom: Dara Shikoh, eldest son of the Mogul emperor Shah Jahan, conversing with representatives of various religions.

sayings of the Prophet and to those of his family members and companions; and *ahar* (plural *athar*: "trace, vestige"), which is used for the sayings of the companions and followers and only rarely for the sayings of the Prophet. However, many Hadith were fabricated by sects, factions, and other groups as ways to validate their interests. Thus arose a "science of the Hadith" to distinguish the genuine from the false. One of the greatest Muslim theologians, the Arabic scholar al-Bukhari (named for his birthplace, Bukhara; d. 870), chose to write about only 2,762 of the 20,000 Hadith in circulation at his time; a selection that fanatics refused to accept. Even so, his work, entitled *Sahih* and also called *al'Jama al'Sahih* (The Authentic Sunna), has remained the

and to spot errors. In truth, two versions of the sacred text exist, although they differ very little: that of Afs al Asim (the "standard") and that of Warsh al-Nafi. The definitive text used in editions today was first published in Egypt after World War II.

At the same time, progress was being made in philosophical research, in the style of the Greek texts, the translations of Plato and Aristotle, leading to the first misunderstandings between philosophical spirit and theological rigidity. The Hadith—the sayings of the Prophet and his companions—serve to verify the more obscure passages of the Koran on the basis of the actions and opinions of the Prophet. In the Arabic language the noun *hadith* means "story, speech, report, account." The Hadith are supplementary to the Koran because they provide the "Tradition," based on the acts, words, and behaviors of the Prophet Muhammad, along with his tacit consent to words spoken in his presence. The word is etymologically derived from an ancient adjective meaning "recent, news, novelties." Other terms used are *khabar* (news, information), applied to both the

basis of research of the Hadith (another five similar texts are considered to be equally valid).

The Hadith are arranged on a scale of forty-four values according to the level of their reliability, but all of them, even those that are unacceptable for obvious reasons (such as references to events that took place after the death of the Prophet), are part of the *Sunna*. The school of study based on the theological studies made at Mecca is called Sunnite, that which prefers to follow the theological studies made at Medina is called Malikite, and that which is based exclusively on the behavior of Ali and the "impeccable" Alid imams is called Shiite.

There are then the three sciences of *Shari'a* (Islam's religious law): the science of sources or methodological bases (*Ilm al-Usul*), the science of theological-philosophical principles (*Ilm Usul al-Din*), and the science of the means of transmission and the application of the traditions (*Ilm al-Ahadith*).

Differences in method led to the formation of four schools of Muslim law in Sunnism (Hanafi, Maliki, Shafi'i, Hanbali) and to three trends in Shiism (Zaydi, Ghulat or Mutualita, Imami). The Shiites have different interpretations of certain verses of the Koran, and some of their readings differ in syntax and terminology from those of the Sunnite.

Muslim Holidays

• **Laylat al-Qadr** *The "night of power or destiny," 27 Ramadan. More beautiful than a thousand months; therein descend the angels and the spirit by permission of God for every matter. A night of peace until the rising of the dawn (Koran 97:3–5). Muslims spend the night reading the Koran and praying.*

• **Id al-Fitr** *The "feast of breaking the fast," held on the first day of the month of Sawwal. Once considered the least important holiday, it is today looked upon as the most joyous, with the exchange of greetings, gifts, and thanks to God for making it through the month of Ramadan. Wearing new clothes, the faithful go to the mosque to pray (this holiday unites the largest number of the faithful). Muslims visit relatives and enjoy large banquets, part of which is given to the poor. Any differences among friends and relatives are resolved so as to begin a happy life.*

• **Mawlid al-Nabi** *The birthday of the Prophet, on 12 First Rabi. Celebration of this holiday began in the tenth century. The day is very important for Sufis, for whom it culminates the celebrations begun on the first day of First Rabi. The Prophet's life is read and eulogies are spoken.*

• **Laylat al-Mir'aj** *The Night of the Ascension, 27 Rajab. This holiday commemorates the Prophet's nocturnal vision. The day is spent in prayer with readings about the*

mi'raj and the life of the Prophet.

• **Id al-Adha** *The "feast of the sacrifice," 10 Du al-Hijjah. An obligatory holiday, its celebration usually lasts three days. It commemorates the sacrifice of the ram by the prophet Abraham, who had been about to sacrifice his firstborn son, Ishmael, to God. The episode is also commemorated on the last day of the pilgrimage to Mecca. Muslims say group prayers and then sacrifice an animal, one third of which is distributed to the poor.*

Three other optional holidays:

• *The last Friday of Ramadan, with prayers in the mosque.*

• *Laylat al-Bara'h (Shab i-Barat), 15 Shaban, the day (or night) of forgiveness, a review of what has happened to human beings during the year (particularly popular among Indian Muslims).*

• *Ashura, 10 Muharram, the day on which Noah left the Ark, Moses and the Jews left Egypt, and Husein suffered martyrdom at Karbala at the hands of the Umayyads. Particularly popular among Shiites.*

There are also:

• *The first of Muharram, day of the hegira, the "emigration" of the Prophet from Mecca and the beginning of the Muslim year.*

• *The month of Ramadan.*

THE BIRTH OF SUFISM

Every religion awakens a mystical search in the souls of those who are thirsty for God and ready to drink from the fountain of light far from bureaucratic restrictions. The unfortunate reality is that all religions can at times seem to offer only a restricted view, based on rigid rules and standards of worship.

The rich world of the Near and Middle East, heir to Alexandrian, Roman, Byzantine, and Sassanian-Parthian splendors, offered multiple cultural possibilities to those within Islam who were seeking to unify a mystical-ascetic yearning with a mono-

Right: Window of the tomb of Agi Bektash, Cappadocia, Turkey.

Left: A wise Sufi, miniature by Reza Abbasi, Isfahan, 1634.

Below: Tomb of the Sufi master Seyid Bakuvi, fifteenth century, Baku, Azerbaijan.

and not completely formulated way of Sufism. There were other, less-dignified forms of "spiritual seeking." All of these existed side by side, sometimes blending, sometimes clashing with one another. There were those who were not drawn to the contemplative path and preferred instead a more active and involved path of action. Such persons could choose to live in one of the fortified monasteries located

lithic syncretism. Those who wished to flee the consumerism of the time and the quest for earthly honors, seeking instead the affirmation of the spirit, could choose among several routes. There was that of the ascetics (*nussak; zuhhad,* singular *zahid,* from *zuhd,* "to renounce"), that of the penitents (*nasikun*), that of the wandering preachers (*qussas*), the way of condemnation (*malamatiyya,* or *malamiyya*), or the vague

like outposts along the frontier of Islam. In those places they could lead the life of spiritual asceticism of a "monk in arms." Or they could choose to join the *Futuwwa* (youth and chivalry), an Islamic brotherhood of artisan guilds that promoted aesthetic and altruistic ideals and put concern for the well-being of one's neighbor ahead of concern for one's self.

From the historical point of view, antecedents to Sufism can be found in the Arab colonies of Basra and Kufa. The first, rational and realistic, had five important masters, each with many followers; the second, more liberal, with a Shiite and Neoplatonist outlook, had seven masters, and they laid the basis for

the mystical school of Baghdad in the ninth century.

Thus, from the very beginning Islam has had a mystical side, and it may represent the historical basis of Sufism, which at its appearance was already accompanied by the mystical current of the Malamatiyya, mentioned above. The distinction between Malamati and Sufi was made by the same Sufi writers who compiled the various histories of Sufism. For Jami (1414–1492), "There is a difference between the *abd* (the servant, the devout, first level), the *khadim* (the zealot, the religious servant, second level), the *faqir* (the pauper, third level), and the *zahid* (the ascetic, 'he who senses disgust,' the fourth level). A *malamati* can pass through these four levels, but not surpass them, much like a *qalandar* (dervish). After these there are the *mutasawwif:* the Sufi 'on the way,' but not complete because of earthly ambitions. Last is the Sufi who passes through all these levels to then overcome them because his single goal is God." Within the Muslim sphere, no interest has been given to seeking out the "origins" of Sufism: at a certain moment it existed, nothing more. It has been Western scholars over the last two centuries who have tried to track down its probable derivations, but they have not always done so with

Above: Graves of the Naqshbandiyya *tariqa* at Vartacen, Azerbaijan.

Right: A Sufi *dergah* (dervish retreat), from the *Menazilnameh* by Matrakji, sixteenth century, Topkapi Palace Library, Istanbul.

Opposite top: A gathering of Sufis in the *Diwan* of Amir Dihlawi, Iran, eighteenth century.

Opposite bottom: Entry to the Sulamiyya *dergah* at San'a, Yemen.

the level of objectivity required of a researcher.

Put simply, Christian, Indian, Zoroastrian, and other ascetic forms are what Western historiography has found, concerned as it was with establishing the possible derivations and probable interchanges between Christianity and Islam, while showing almost no interest in the religions that preceded Islam in the countries of central and eastern Asia and that thus may have influenced it. This vast area of Asia was inhabited by Turkish tribes, and the Turks are known for their interest in all formulations of religious truth. Buddhism, for example, spread in China thanks to the Turkish kingdoms in northern China, in particular the Wei (386–551). Loyang, capital of the Tabgac Turks, had more than 1,300 pagodas, and on the orders of Thopa Hong II (471–499), masterpieces of Buddhist art were created in the caves of Longmen. These were of Greco-Roman inspiration, following models imported from Gandhara, where other Turks had made them, thus laying the basis for the Buddhist iconography.

One must remember that Buddhism was an elitist religion that was expressed primarily in the direction of a well-organized and powerful monastic order. It is not beyond the realm of the possible that when the Turkish intelligentsia went from Buddhism

to Islam, the Buddhist monastic class slowly flowed into what can be called Islamic monasticism. The Muslim mystical movement called the Qalandariyya appeared in Khorasan early in the eleventh century as a Sufi order, with many Buddhist monks among its members. It was further influenced by Buddhism in the course of the thirteenth century, and only after its spread to the West by Savi (d. 1232) did it come into full alignment with *Shari'a*.

Thus two worlds must be spoken of in the formation of Sufism. One is connected to the occult philosophies that originated in the classical period of the West; the other is the shamanistic, Indian, and Buddhist world of the East.

in poetry over the past several centuries (in Arabic, Persian, and Turkish, but also in the other languages of the vast Islamic world, thanks to the presence of Sufi poets, thus giving it depth and historical authenticity). Developments in the sciences occurred both because leading scientists were Sufi masters (as, for example, Avicenna, of central

THE IMPORTANCE OF SUFISM IN ISLAM

Sufism had a significant effect on the Islamic world. A sense of this importance is provided by several lines from one of the leading Muslim philosophers of the twentieth century, Seyyed Hossein Nasr: "To fully express the teachings of Sufism one must present at least a summary of Sufi doctrine, including metaphysics, meaning the study of the beginning and nature of things; cosmology, in terms of the structure of the universe and multiple states of being; traditional psychology, which includes one of the most profound forms of psychotherapy; and finally eschatology, which concerns the final scope of man and the universe and the posthumous future of man. An exposition of Sufi teaching should also include treatment of its spiritual methods, their application, and the way in which they take root in the very soul of the disciple."

Sufism has been responsible for developments

The Major Sufi Confraternities

Because of its open-minded character and the influence of great masters, Sufism has seen the creation of many confraternities and related branches over the course of the centuries. Many of these are still active; others, for a variety of reasons, have declined. The following are some of the best known of the 124 active confraternities.
Qadiriyya *Founded by Abd al-Qadir al-Jilani (d. 1166); its main chapter is in Baghdad, with many branches.*
Rifa'iyya *Founded in Iraq by Ahmad al-Rifa'i (d. 1175), with numerous ramifications.*
Chishtiyya *Of Afghan-Indian origin, founded in the thirteenth century, with its headquarters at Ajmer, India.*
Mawlawiyya *(Mevlevi) Founded by Jalal al-Din Rumi (d. 1273), it is well known in the West because of the* sema, *danced by the so-called whirling dervishes.*
Jerrahiyya-Khalwatiyya *(Jerrahi-Halveti) Branch of the Suhrawardiyya, later the Khalwatiyya, founded in Khorasan by Zahir al-Din (d. 1397); brought to Istanbul by Nur al-Din al-Jerrahi in 1704.*
Naqshbandiyya *Founded at Bukhara by Abd al-Ghujdawani (d. 1220), then by Muhammad al-Naqshbandi (1318–1389). This* tariqa *is known for political involvement and helped Islam survive in countries where Communism sought to eradicate it.*

importance to European medicine) and because the sciences were taught in universities, institutions that were founded by Sufis (the world's oldest still-active university is the Islamic university of Al-Azhar in Cairo). The leading architects in the world of Islam were Sufi masters, as were the leading calligraphers and the most important miniaturists, musicians, sociologists, and psychoanalysts.

Aside from poetry—which in general contains images related to various spiritual states (*ahwal*, singular *hal*) of the soul in its search for the divine—there are numerous prose works, some more clearly doctrinal, others more practical, others descriptive, presenting a model to follow rather than giving immediate instructions. Sufi literature—most of all in Arabic and Persian but also in the many other languages of the Muslim people, such as Turkish, Urdu, Bengali, and Sindhi—is like a vast ocean whose currents move in different directions and with different forms but that always return to the pure and simple element from which they arose.

To return to Seyyed Hossein Nasr: "Also in the field of instruction, Sufism has had a profound effect, since its fundamental purpose is the total education of man in order to make him reach the full and perfect realization of all his abilities. The direct participation of many Sufis (for example, the

Seljuk minister Khwajah Nizam al-Mulk) in the foundation of universities and madrasas (university faculties), as well as the role performed by Sufi centers in the diffusion of education, make the influence of Sufism inseparable from the cultural development of Islam. And again: during those times and in those

Opposite: A *tashbi* (Muslim rosary) of 990 beads, Konya, Turkey.

Above: Tomb of Jalal al-Din Rumi, Konya, Turkey.

Right: Three Sufi Mevlevi, the so-called whirling dervishes.

The Ninety-nine Names of God in the Koran

According to Muslim theology, there are four thousand names of God, meaning vocalized representations of his attributes. One thousand of these are known only to God; one thousand are known to God and the angels; one thousand to God, the angels, and the prophets; and one thousand to God, the angels, the prophets, and the believers. Of this last thousand, three hundred are mentioned in the Pentateuch, three hundred in the Psalms, three hundred in the Gospels, and one hundred in the Koran. Of this hundred, ninety-nine are known to the ordinary faithful, while one is hidden, secret, and accessible only to the most illuminated mystics.

The Koran refers to the ninety-nine names ("name": *ism*; plural, *osama* or *asamy*):
"Most excellent titles hath God [*al-Asma al-Husna*]: by these call ye on Him and stand aloof from those who pervert his titles" (8:180).

Below: *Tashbi* (Muslim rosary) of ninety-nine beads.

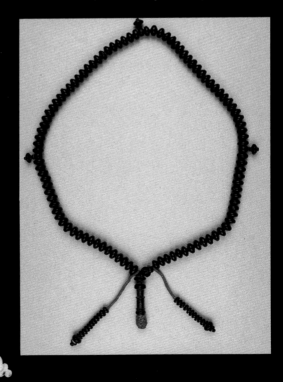

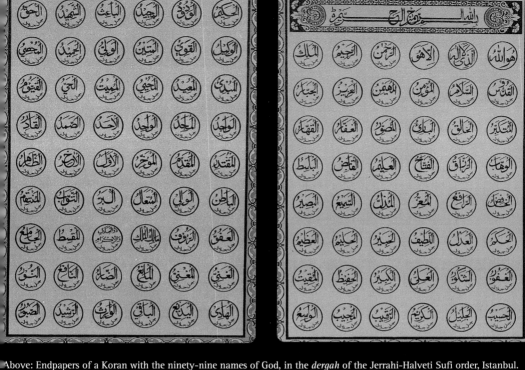
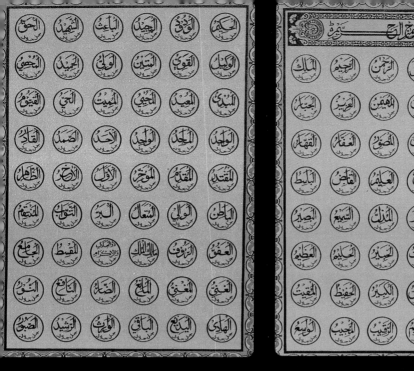

Above: Endpapers of a Koran with the ninety-nine names of God, in the *dergah* of the Jerrahi-Halveti Sufi order, Istanbul.

Call upon "God," or call upon the "God of Mercy," by whichsoever ye will invoke him: he hath most excellent names (17:110).

God! There is no God but he! Most excellent his titles! (20:8).

The Prophet Muhammad said, "There are ninety-nine names that belong only to God. He that learns them, understands them, and enumerates them enters Paradise and achieves eternal salvation." The mystic Tosun Bayrak, sheikh of the Jerrahiyya-Khalwatiyya Sufi order: "The beautiful names of God are proof of the existence of the oneness of God. O you who are parched and troubled because of the weight of suffering of the material world, may God let his beautiful names be a soothing balm for your wounded hearts. Learn, understand, and recite the beautiful names of God. Seek out signs of these attributes of God in the skies, on the earth, and in what is beautiful about you yourselves. In that way you

will find favor, in accordance with the measure of your sincerity. With the permission of God, those who have doubts will find certainty, the ignorant will find knowledge, those who deny will find affirmation. The greedy will become generous, tyrants will bow their heads, and the fire in the heart of the envious will go out." Understanding the "essence" of these attributes calms the soul and brings faith and spiritual enrichment. For this reason, on a purely practical level, it has been the habit to repeat the names while counting the beads of a rosary composed of ninety-nine beads (or thirty-three if done three times). This rosary, called a *subha* in Arabic and *tashbi* (or *komboloy*) in Turkish, may have been derived from those used by Buddhists, composed of 108 beads and used in central and eastern Asia since the fourth century. In turn, the Muslim rosary, through imitation, led to the Catholic rosary, which was adopted at the end of the twelfth century and later given its current form

It is no coincidence that the texts of the most elevated quality and beauty are those written by Sufis!"

Many of the principal Muslim architects are connected to Sufism by way of symbolism and the golden section; many masters of calligraphy and many miniaturists belonged to a Sufi order. As for music, it was considered legitimate in Islam and, at an early time, was permitted only in the form of the spiritual concert (*sema*), which is a distinctly Sufi concept, and the tradition of Arabic, Iranian, and Turkish classical music has been cultivated over the centuries most of all by Sufis; certain developments in Indian music are directly related to the practice of Sufism.

The Sufis have been cultivators of the arts in part because Sufism means becoming more aware of the divine beauty that is manifest everywhere, since as the Prophet says: *Inna Allah jamil yuhibbu al-Jamal* ("Certainly, God is beautiful and loves beauty"). Finally, it should be pointed out that the Western world's interest in Sufism has led to an increase in associations of "false Sufis," not unlike the myriad false gurus and faith healers of the New Age. Such associations arise because of the interest in age-old traditions, but such traditions cannot be understood or accepted without authentic, constant, and profound dedication.

places where the traditional educational system has been destroyed—as for example following the Mongol invasions—Sufi centers were the only repositories of official and academic knowledge; it was on the basis of their knowledge that the traditional schools were reconstructed.

"In the sector of the sciences and arts the influence of Sufis has been enormous. In Islam, the tradition of Sufism is closely connected to the development of the sciences, including the natural sciences. In almost all forms of art, from poetry to architecture, the affinity with Sufism is particularly strong. Even while in this life Sufis live as in the pronaos to Paradise, and therefore they breathe a climate of spiritual splendor whose beauty is reflected in all they say and do. For Islam itself the Divinity is beauty, and for Sufism, which constitutes the marrow of Islam and contains all its essence, this peculiarity appears particularly marked.

MUHAMMAD AND SCIENCE

The theologian Abu Zakariya al-Nawawi (1233–1277) collected *Forty Sayings of the Prophet*, the thirty-sixth of which says, "God shows mercy on his servant if his servant shows mercy on his brother. For he who opens the way to knowledge in a science, God will open the way to Paradise." In another Hadith, Muhammad says, "Seek knowledge, even if you must go to China to find it." The Koran itself calls on believers to study. Islam promotes the sciences, and since the earliest times, medicine, astronomy, physics, chemistry, psychology–every field of research–has been brought to a high level that provided the base of scientific knowledge in Europe centuries later.

According to an old Arab saying, the glory of God is written in the book of the skies. The glory of Islam is written in books about the sky: most of the names of the heavenly bodies and the related technical terms are Arabic, such as Betelgeuse (*Bayt al-Jawzah*), Altair (*al-Ta'ir*), Deneb (*dhanab*), Pherkad (*farad*), azimuth (*al-Summut*), nadir (*nazir*), and zenith (*alzamt*). As early as the beginning of the ninth century the caliph al-Mam'un had an observatory built at Baghdad. In the tenth century Islamic astrolabes (*asturlab*) became widespread even in Europe and were described by Gerbert of Aurillac (ca. 930–1003), who, after studying mathematics and astronomy at Muslim schools in Spain, became Pope Sylvester II. It may have been the Chinese who discovered the properties of the magnetic needle, but it was the Muslims who were first to apply the principles, discover-

Above: Iranian astrolabe of the fifteenth century.

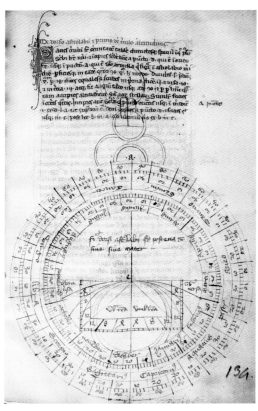

Opposite top: A *sema* before King Ghazan of Transoxiana, miniature from 1318.

Opposite bottom: A *kashgol* (bowl for alms) of the Nimatalla Sufis, fifteenth century.

Right: Translation of the *Study of the Astrolabe* by Fakraddin Karki, fourteenth-century Italian codex, National Library, Naples.

The Andalusian geographer Abdullah al-Idrisi (1100–1166) put together a monumental compilation of information about the Earth for Roger II, the Norman king of Sicily, the *Kitab al-Rujar* (*The Book of Roger*), in which, well before Galileo, he spoke of the spherical nature of the Earth, revolving around the Sun with the other planets. The great Persian poet and mathematician Omar Khayyam (d. 1123), best known for his *Rubaiyat*, was the first to solve cubic equations, providing both algebraic and geometric solutions.

There was then the astronomical school and observatory of Maragheh, northwest Iran, founded in the thirteenth century by Nasir al-Tusi and imitated in Tabriz and Damascus. The greatest Islamic astronomer was the Timurid ruler and astronomer Ulug-Beg, who established an astronomical observatory at Samarkand in 1420, which trained numerous astronomers. The last important Muslim observatory was that built by Taqi al-Din at Istanbul between 1575 and 1577, which was followed by similar observatories in India.

ing the compass. Abu Abd-Allah al-Battani (ca. 858–929) measured the angle of the ecliptic, the duration of the tropical year, the orbit of the Sun, and the circumference of the Earth with a variance of only twenty-four seconds compared to today's measurement. The Persian astronomer and mathematician al-Khuwarizmi (d. 850) elaborated the first algorithms and algebra, both of which bear Arabic names (*algorithm* and *algorism* are derived from his name); he wrote a treatise, *The Shape of the Earth*, translations of which were later burned on pyres in Europe.

Abd al-Wafah (d. 998) developed trigonometry and the geometry of the sphere and discovered the variations of lunar movement; five hundred years before Galileo (1564–1642), the Iranian Abu al-Rayhan al-Biruni (973–1050), author of 103 great works on various sciences, studied the rotation of the Earth.

These astronomical studies were accompanied by similar work in the field of geography, which became a highly important branch of Islamic science. In the mid-ninth century, Abu Yusuf al-Kindi (d. 874) wrote hundreds of treatises on a variety of subjects; he was later well known to Christian scholars of the Middle Ages. The works of Ibn Khurradadhbih (ca. 846), which refer to both Korea and Japan, served as the basis for later geographers. During the first years of the tenth century, Ahmad ibn Fadlan provided the first descriptions of the Volga and the Caspian Sea, along with descriptions of Uzbekistan. The eleventh century was dominated by the figure of al-Biruni; the fourteenth by that of Ibn Battuta (1304–1377), who traveled to China, Sri Lanka, central Asia, Nigeria, and the Byzantine territories. *The Geographical Dictionary,* compiled by al-Hamawi Yaqut (1179–1229), listed in alphabetical order all the known cities and lands, giving physical measurements, climate notes, and political and cultural information, in many ways anticipating today's atlases.

The outstanding figure of the fifteenth century was Shihab ibn Majid, the author of works in prose and poetry, as well as an important navigator. In his twenty-two principal works he deals with the phases of the moon, the compass, and the Red Sea and Indian Ocean. He led Vasco da Gama—who called him Malemo Canaza (from the Arabic *mu'allim kanaka,* "master of nautical astrology")—from Malindi in Africa to Calicut in India.

A highly famous figure at the end of the fifteenth century was the Turkish admiral Piri Re'is (1473–1554), who in 1513 completed a *Great Atlas of the World,* in large part displayed at the Topkapi Palace Library in Istanbul, which includes detailed maps of the coasts of America.

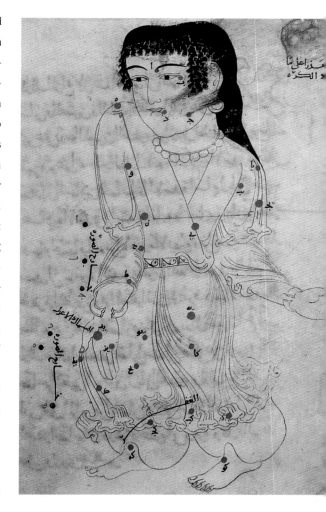

PRACTICAL SCIENCES AND THE PRACTICE OF SCIENCES

Islam also made great contributions to the fields of chemistry, mathematics, optics, botany, and the development of technology, the social sciences, and music. Indeed, the scientific method itself was introduced by Muslims, while the field of medicine

Opposite top: "The Imperial House of the Astronomers," miniature, 1418, University Library, Istanbul.
Opposite bottom: The great armillary sphere of Murad III, 1581, University Library, Istanbul.
Above: The constellation of Virgo, Bodleian Library, Oxford.

merits a chapter unto itself.

In mathematics—part of which we have already seen in relation to astronomy—a considerable Islamic contribution was that of Indian numerals and the zero (*sifr*), which are still called Arabic numerals today. These had been in use in the Orient as early as the eighth century, while the Christian West continued to use Roman numerals until the twelfth century. The history of European mathematics can be said to begin with Leonardo Fibonacci (ca. 1170–1240), the Italian mathematician also known as Leonardo da Pisa, who studied with an Arab master and advocated the use of Arabic notation.

The mathematician and physicist Ibn al-Haytham (965–1039), also known as Alhazen, was a great pioneer in optics. He experimented with twenty-seven different types of lenses, and discovered the laws of refraction and that the eye reflects rays. His *Kitab fi al-Manazr* (published in 1572 at Basil, Switzerland, under the title *Thesaurus Opticus*) was important to such scientists as Bacon, da Vinci, Kepler, and Newton.

In the field of chemistry, the great Arab alchemist and physician Jabir ibn Hayyan al-Sufi (d. 813), also known as Geber, invented the distillation of water and many types of laboratory equipment. He identified many salts, alkalines, and acids; produced sulfuric acid, caustic soda, and turpentine; and discovered mercury. He should not be confused with Abu Marwan ibn Hayyan (987–1076), a great historian during the Middle Ages.

The Iranian Abu Bakr al-Razi (ca. 854–935), director

Left: Ottoman observatory in the eighteenth century, Topkapi Palace Library, Istanbul.
Opposite top: Noria waterwheel at Hama, on the Orontes River, Syria.
Opposite bottom: The genealogical tree of Murad IV, Ambrosian Library, Milan.

of the hospital of Rayy, philosopher, physician, and chemist, classified the chemical substances and determined that the functions of the human body are based on complex chemical reactions. The Spaniard Maslama al-Majriti (954–1007), mathematician, astronomer, and chemist, demonstrated the principle of the chemical preservation of mass, presented in Europe by Lavoisier about 900 years later.

The following terms are taken from the Arabic language: chemistry (*al-kymia*), alcohol (*al-kuhul*), alkali and alkaline (*al-qili*), arsenic (*al-zirnih*), aphta, antimony, alembic, realgar, and aludel. Related to Islamic techniques are the distillation of rose water, perfumes, and essential oils; the distillation of crude oil; the extraction of industrial oils and fats for the preparation of acids; and the manufacture of soap, glass, ceramics, inks, dyes, and metal alloys (hence the fame of swords from Damascus and Toledo). Both

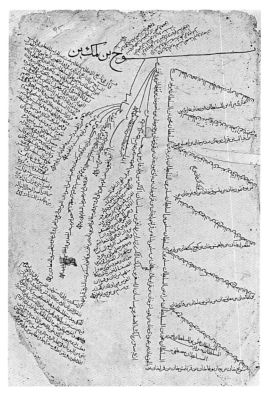

julep and *syrup* come to us directly from the Arabic. Al-Gazari proposed the method of experimental verification and established the width of calipers; Giabir made the first varnish for commercial use; and several colors, such as lilac (*laylak*), carmine red, and crimson (*qirmizi*), were introduced to Europe from the Islamic world. Several irrigation techniques were introduced to Europe from Islamic countries, such as the kind of waterwheel known as a noria (*na'ura*) or Persian wheel, the windmill, underground tubes (*qanat*), and various machines that make use of gears, first among them the water clock. Several food plants, along with the methods of cultivation associated with them, were introduced to Europe from the Muslims, including the sesame, carob (*kharrub*), millet, rice, lemons (*laymun*), melons, apricots (*al-berquq*), scallions (from Ascalon, the seaport in southern Palestine), aloe, ginger, and most of all sugar (*sukkar*). There is then the creation of special fabrics: muslin (from Mosul, Iraq), damask (Damascus), and satin (Arabic *zaytun*, from Zaitun, the town in China where it was produced).

The Knights Templars, and most of all the Crusades, were behind a great many of these exchanges. There was also the center of Andalusia in Muslim Spain, which was visited by a host of Christian scholars. All this cultural fervor is related to the Islamic culture of the book, which was among the most active, and a love for writing that made Islamic calligraphy a noble art, almost superior to painting itself: an art that can be fully appreciated if it is understood as a kind of music, for like

music it has rules of composition, rhythm, harmony, and counterpoint that are most rewarding to those with a well-trained eye and an aesthetic passion. Islamic writing has developed from the imperfect forms of its primitive beginning to an art form replete with a variety of different "hands" (meaning styles or characters) and traits (lines, spaces, bodies, and other graphic arrangements).

This passion for writing, which was found throughout the Muslim world from the very earliest times, is related to the important subject of paper, which was invented by the Chinese along with printing in the first century AD; it was

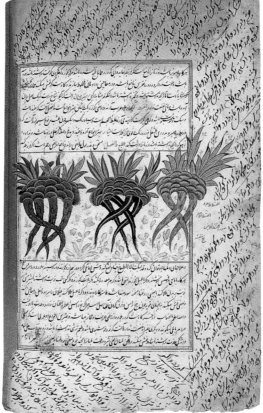

known and largely used in Islamic countries as early as the conquest of Samarkand in 751. From the Islamic world it then spread to Europe, a memory of which remains in the fact that a quantity of paper is still called a *ream*, from the Arabic *rizmah* (bundle). As early as 1040, merchants in Cairo were wrapping their goods in sheets of paper.

Although known and occasionally put to use since the ninth century, printing attracted little

According to al-Ya'qubi, during the tenth century, the suburb of Baghdad called al-Waddad alone had 118 bookshops, the most famous being that of the philosopher Ibn al-Nadim (d. 990). The oldest series-made manuscript dates to 874, by which time authors were being paid a percent of the sale of their works.

Libraries were also of great importance, the most famous being the Bayt al-Hikma (House of Wis-

Opposite, top and bottom: Three pages from the *Greek Herbal (Kitab al-Hashaish)* by Dioscorides, Isfahan, 1658, Academy of Sciences, St. Petersburg.

Right: *Treatise on Astronomy*, seventeenth century, Ambrosian Library, Milan.

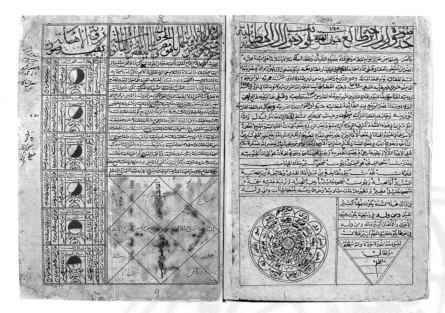

interest, since so much preference was given to the manuscript book. Because of the highly organized guilds of scribes (*warraqin*), the cost of producing a manuscript book and the time involved did not provide incentives for the art of typography. During the tenth century, the artisan workshop in Baghdad of Abd-Allah Abu Said al-Mullah had so many scribes that it could copy and bind twelve copies of a 164-page manuscript in one day. The warraqin set up their workshops in the largest cities: Baghdad, Cairo, Damascus, Granada, Fez, Bukhara, Samarkand, and Córdoba.

dom), set up in Baghdad by the caliph al-Mam'un in 815, followed by the Nizamiyya (1065) and the Mustansiriyya (1227). In Cairo the Khizanah al-Kutub contained 1.6 million books arranged in forty rooms, all with open shelves. This led to a science of classification and the compilation of reference works, bibliographic works, dictionaries, guides, and large "encyclopedias," some of which were composed of a great many volumes, such as the famous *Rasa'il Ikhwan al-Safa khillan al-Wafa*, compiled by the "Brothers of Purity" in a format anticipating Diderot's *Encyclopédie*.

MEDICINE AND ISLAM

Islamic medicine is the result of a synthesis of the methods of Hippocrates and Galen (exercised primarily in Alexandria) and Iranian and Indian medicine (from the Sassanid city of Gundishapur, a principal cultural center of the late classical period). To this was grafted the so-called Medicine of the Prophet (*Tibb al-Nabi*), which was based on the sayings of Muhammad and passages in the Koran. Baghdad soon became the primary center of this knowledge, with a series of translations of the ancient codices of the various schools and from the Greek, Pahlavi, and Sanskrit languages. At the same time the basis was laid for medicine's technical vocabulary.

Left: Maimonides. Above: A doctor bleeds a patient with a cupping glass, from the *Maqamat* of al-Hariri, Iraq, 1240, Academy of Sciences, St. Petersburg.

Opposite top: The *Kitab al-Hayawan* (*Book of Zoology*) by al-Jahiz. Opposite bottom: *Bestiary* by Ibn Bakhtishu, Maragheh, 1298, Morgan Library, New York.

The second large Islamic contribution to medicine was the institution of the hospital (in Arabic *bimaristan* or *maristan*, from *bimar*, "sick," or from *dar al'marda*) and, with it, the mental asylum. The first hospital was created in 707 at Damascus by the caliph al-Walid Mansuri and is still active today. The Nuri hospital, founded in Damascus during the twelfth century, was famous throughout the Islamic world.

In 821 the Abbasid governor of Khorasan wrote to his son that there were numerous hospitals in the Turko-Iranian region. From 790 on, the medical capital was Baghdad, which then had ten hospitals; two centuries later—as Ibn Fadlan wrote—these had grown to sixty, each with pharmacies and libraries, some open to the public, and various specialized departments. In 832 the seventh Abbasid caliph, Harun al-Rashid, added a large faculty of medicine to the *Bayt al-Hikma* (House of Wisdom) in Baghdad. The faculty published a weekly case report and had special sections for the mentally disturbed.

The first mental asylum was founded by Nur al-Din Mahmud Zaniji at Aleppo a little after 1157. Rearranged in 1260 by the Mameluke al-Nasir, it was divided in three sections: early stages, care, and chronic cases. Another important asylum was in the Turkish city of Divrigi, founded in 1228 by Princess Turan Malk. Another notable asylum was that of Edirne, former capital of the Ottoman Empire, which Beyazid II had constructed between 1488 and 1498. The seventeenth-century Turkish historian Eviliya Çelebi wrote that musical therapy was among the treatments practiced.

Then came some of the outstanding figures of Islamic medicine. The first important work—the *Firdaus al-Hikma* (*The Paradise of Knowledge*)—was written by Ali al-Tabari in 850. His disciple, the Iranian Abu Bakr Muhammad al-Razi (ca. 854–925), from Rayy, one of the leading clinics of the time, was skilled at the analysis of symptoms

and the prognosis of diseases and was a leader in pathological anatomy. Founder of obstetrics, he was the first to describe smallpox and measles and created the clinic in the modern sense of the word. One of his best-known texts, *Kitab al-Hawi fi al-Tibb* (widespread in Europe under the title *Continens* and printed at Brescia in 1486) is the most voluminous work in the Arabic language. It includes four chapters on psychiatry, along with a study on the placebo effect and psychosomatic medicine. Twenty chapters of his *Sira al-Falsafiyya* (*Spiritual Medicine*) deal with psychiatry. His major work is a treatise on smallpox and the plague. He was followed by the Iranian Ali ibn al Abbas al-Majusi (906–995), author of the *Kitab al-Maliki* (*Liber Regius*), a work of considerable clinical accuracy.

All these eminent physicians were eclipsed by the Persian Ibn Sina, called Avicenna in the West, and by his *Canon of Medicine,* doubtless the most read, most influential, and most used clinical work from 1100 to 1500. Avicenna was born in 980 at Afshana, near Bukhara, in today's Uzbekistan, and died in 1037. He discovered the systems of tuberculosis and diabetes, studied human psychology in depth, and formulated the basis for the correct understanding of the functions of the human body. His *Canon,* composed of fourteen volumes dealing with five subjects, was still being used as a textbook in the universities of Christian Europe in the eighteenth century. It has chapters on frenzy, delirium, lethargy, apathy, and melancholy. He accurately distinguished anxiety from depression and provided basic instructions for the treatment of epilepsy.

The first accurate description of the circulation of blood was written by Ibn al-Nafis (d. 1288), who published a medical encyclopedia (*al-Kitab al-Shalil fi al-Tibb*) in three hundred sections and *Epitome of the Canon*. The same level of knowledge was not reached in Europe until the seventeenth century.

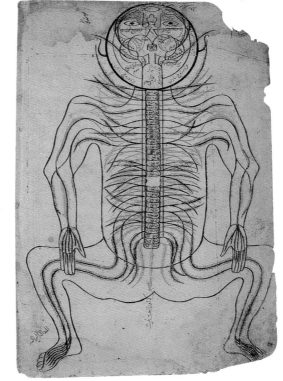

Another important contribution is related to ophthalmology; indeed, both *retina* and *cataract* are derived from the Arabic. The first important author in this field was al-Ibadi (d. 873). In the tenth century, Ali ibn Isa al-Kahhal, the best known and most important ophthalmologist, wrote the *Tadhkirat al-Kahhalin* (*Notebook of the Ophthalmologist*). Further discoveries in this field were made by the Iraqi Ammar al-Mawsili in the eleventh century.

The Andalusian al-Katib wrote a treatise on gynecology in the tenth or eleventh century. Abu Khasim (d. ca. 1013), known as Abulcasis (his works were translated by Gherardo of Cremona), was the leading Muslim surgeon. His major work, a detailed account of surgery known as the *Tasrif* (*The Collection*), was for many years the leading surgical textbook. By the tenth century all types of surgical instruments were being made in the Islamic world, complex and specially designed. Seville saw the activity of the Ibn Zuhr family of outstanding physicians, known for open-heart operations; in Iran, the best-known physicians after Avicenna were Ismail al-Jurjani (d. 1136), a great encyclopedist of medical science, and the Turk Qutb al-Din Shirazi (1236–1311), a commentator on the *Canon*, both of whom moved with great technical mastery from cataract operations to those for gallstones. Many other doctors made great strides in veterinary science.

Many of these outstanding physicians were also chemists, philosophers, and sometimes also astronomers, and all of them belonged to Sufi confraternities (see the list on page 94).

There is then the highly important area of pharmacology. According to Professor Domenico De Maio, former head of psychiatry at Milan's Fatebenefratelli clinic, "This was the most thoroughly explored branch of Islamic science and certainly got the lion's share, with more than 600,000 manuscripts distributed in all the libraries of the world. It is outstanding for these three reasons: absence of superstition; comparison over vast areas and acceptance of all the types of medicine extraneous to Islam; and the etymological and botanical study of products, the theory of 'test and test again.' "

This branch of Islamic medicine is particularly rich in treatises and handbooks. Among the 180 works by the Turk Muhammad al-Biruni (ca. 973–

Opposite top: Anatomical drawing, fifteenth century, National Library, Paris. Opposite bottom: Representation of the human body and the signs of the zodiac, from a text by Ibn Habib, Granada, ninth century. Below: The preparation of theriac, miniature from 1199, National Library, Paris.

1048), a prolific mathematician, astronomer, physicist, naturalist, chronologist, linguist, and great Sufi master, was the *Kitab al-Saydala fi al-Tibb*, a pharmacological treatise with synonyms in Syriac, Persian, Greek, Afghan, and Kurdish.

The first important treatise in the field of psychiatry and psychotherapy was written by Najab al-Din Unhammad of Samarkand in the eighth century. This was followed in the eleventh century by the *Risalah fi al-Tibb wa al-Ahdat al-Naf Saniya* by Abu Sa'yd ibn Bukhtyshu, which deals with holism, psychosomatics, and somatopsychism. The most fully described subject in this field was depression, as in the *Kitab al-Azmina* by Ibn Masawayh (793–857), the *Kitab al-Hudud* by Abu al-Ash'ath (886–970), and the *Siwan al-Hikma* by Ishaq ibn Hunayn of 902. Ishaq ibn Imran (d. 970) wrote the *Maqala fi al-Malihuliya* (*Treatise on Melancholy*), which was translated into Latin by the Benedictine monk Constantinus Africanus. The author

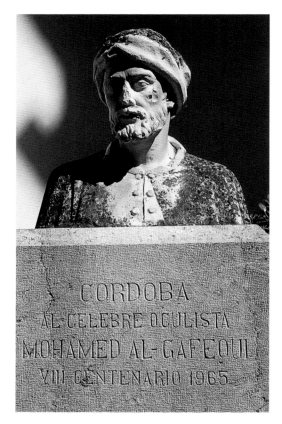

CORDOBA
AL CELEBRE OCULISTA
MOHAMED AL-GAFEQUI
VIII CENTENARIO 1965

distinguished among sorrow, anguish, psychosomatic disturbances, and somatopsychism and dealt with psychotherapy and appropriate medicines.

Islamic medical science continued to make great advances over the centuries even though its progress was seriously blocked by two ill-fated events: the conquests of the Mongols of Genghis Khan in the thirteenth century and European colonial expansion, which dismembered and divided the Islamic states (and, in about two hundred years, the Ottoman Empire).

Left: *The Triumph of Medicine*, miniature, 1199. Above: Muhammad al-Ghafiqi of Córdoba, the greatest oculist of the twelfth century. Opposite top: The courtyard of the university of Al-Azhar at Cairo, in a painting by Ludwig Deutsch (1855–1935). Opposite center: Two Iranian books of the sixteenth century. Opposite bottom: Iranian calligraphy of the nineteenth century.

THE ALPHABET AND CALLIGRAPHY

It would be impossible to fully grasp Islam's scientific research, artistic fervor, and most of all the profound sense of its religious devotion—particularly in the mystical writings—without giving adequate consideration to Arabic writing.

The Phoenician and proto-Arabic alphabets came into being around 1600 BC, derived from the proto-Canaanite. The Phoenician led to the Aramaic, Greek, and proto-Hebrew alphabets, the Parthian, the Palmyrian, and the Nabataean. The Nabataean was the basis of the Arabic alphabet, or more exactly North, or classical, Arabic. Arabic is written from the right to the left; thus an Arabic book begins at what would be the last page in the West.

The first Arabic hand appeared in 632. This was the *kufic*, angular and blocky. By 900 it had been joined by a cursive script, the *naskh*. Guidelines were soon being established for beautiful calligraphy, and the first manuals of rules (*mufraddat*) appeared. The shapes and spacing of individual letters were fixed by Ibn Muqla of Baghdad (d. 940).

During this period two women are known to have excelled in the art of writing: Thana al-Abdulat and Zaineb Shehede, known as Sitta al-Dar.

The efforts of two calligraphers of the Abbasid period—Ibn Bawwab of Baghdad (d. 1022 or 1031) and Yaqut al-Musta'simi (1242–1298)—led to the formation of a famous school of art. Ibn Bawwab defined the width, height, and length of letters using a system of square dots (*noqta*). He also created the *mansub fa'ikh* (*mansub*: "elegant") style; the Iranian school of calligraphy was based on his work. Among his pupils were Muhammad ibn Khazin of Dinawar, who invented the *riq'a* and the *tauqit*; and Khoja Abu Ali, inventor of the *ta'liq*, a style of highly precise cursive writing.

Yaqut al-Musta'simi created the *yaqut* style (a derivation of the *thuluth*) but is best known for introducing the method of trimming the pen nib on a slight slant, giving the writing an oblique angle. This served as the basis of the Turkish calligraphic school, which promoted the "seven classical styles": *muhaqqaq* (compact), *thuluth* (rounded), *naskh* (perfected by Ibn Muqla), *riq'a* (Ottoman chancery), *diwani*, *ta'liq* (Iranian), and *maghribi*. Later added were the *rayhan*, the Iranian *nasta'liq*, introduced to Turkey by Sultan Mehmet II, and the *shikastah*. There were also schools of a local character (the above-mentioned *maghribi* as well as the *andalusi* and *bihari*).

In that way three important centers of calligraphic art came to be recognized: Iran, Turkey, and the Mediterranean.

In Iran, a local hand was originally adopted, the *piramuz* (*kiramiz* in Arabic), of which only a few

very rare examples exist. This gave way to two principal schools, that of Khorasan, founded at Herat by Ja'far ibn Ali (d. ca. 1456), and that to the southwest, represented by Abadal-Rahim al-Khwarezmi. The Indian school was derived from the Iranian and came to present a typical local *naskhi*, vigorous and solid, and a *behari* with a baroque form. The Indian school also came to boast excellent masters, most of all during the Mogul dynasty (also spelled *Mughal* and based on the word *Mongol*, although its founders were Turks; 1526–1857). Outstanding among these masters were Shihab al-Din (twelfth century), Ashraf Khan (d. 1572), and Ja'far Khan. The Chinese Muslims, in direct contact with Afghanistan, Uzbekistan, and India, adopted Arabic writing in a loose, broken style, the *sini*, used most of all in manuscripts made for the Ottoman market.

The Turkish school began with two outstanding masters: Uthman ibn Ali, called Hafiz Othman, whose teaching is still followed today; and the Sufi sheikh Hamd-Allah (1436–1520), also called Hamadullah, who was the author of many treatises and whose students included the Ottoman emperor Beyazid II. The renowned splendor of Turkish calligraphic art is reflected in the popular saying, "The Koran was revealed in Mecca, recited in Egypt, and written in Istanbul."

These two Turkish masters were responsible for the eventual formation of many schools that created far too many great masters to be mentioned here. A particularly characteristic Turkish hand, the *divani*, was developed by Ibrahim Munif. This was a chancery script suitable for a great variety of ornamental uses. Other calligraphic styles, including the traditional, were reworked to create different styles, such as the *shikasteh*, the *skikasteh amiz*, and the *jali*. The *divani jali* variant is also called *humayini*. The *sunbuli* was also later derived from the *divani*.

Aside from these various styles, the Ottoman calligraphers also developed special graphics, such as the *zulf-i'arus* (curl) and the highly functional *siyaqat*; the *gulzar* style, which consists in filling the spaces left open by letters with floral or figurative orna-

Opposite top: Book bound in the seventeenth century, Turkey.
Opposite bottom: Woodcut block for printing, tenth century, Egypt.

Above: The western coasts of South America in a map by the Turkish navigator Piri Re'is (1473–1554).
Below: Scene of Iranian school of the fifteenth century.

ments; the *muthanna* (or *mutanazar*) composition style—also called *aynali* or *ma'kus* (reflection), or *khatt-i muthanna* (facing calligraphy)—which creates a specular image of the writing; the complex and flourishing *tughra* style; and, in particular, the arrangement of words or phrases to form figural compositions, most often zoomorphic, with horses, birds, and lions, but at times also forming faces. In addition to all this, Turkey was home to the almost microscopic style of writing called *ghubar*, or *ghubarari* (powder, powdery). Using this style, Isma'il Abd-Allah, called Ibn al-Zamakjala (d. 1386), wrote the entire text of the Koran (77,934 words) on a single ostrich eggshell; Qasim Ghubari (d. 1624) wrote it on a sheet of paper 21⁵/₈ by 17³/₄ inches; and Mehmet Shefik Bey (d. 1819) wrote it on the ninety-nine beads of a rosary. These are examples of folk art and fall outside the subject of Islamic calligraphy.

ISLAMIC ARCHITECTURE

Islamic buildings make use of two basic elements, the arch and the dome, and also two decorative-constructive elements, the *iwan* (vaulted portal) and *muqarnas* (three-dimensional tiered decorations; the term is derived from the Greek *koronis*: "cornice"). Islamic buildings follow typologies based on their function (e.g., mosque, madrasa, palace, hospital, caravansary, mausoleum, Turkish bath, open market), and some of these typologies involve

specific elements, such as the mihrab and the minbar of the mosque. Many mosques possess an element that has become typical and emblematic of Islam itself: the minaret, a unique feature that rises above a structure and which is usually firmly tied to the ground, united to the environment in which it is located, and is most often organized like a garden. Also typical are the Turkish palaces (for example, the Topkapi Palace of Istanbul, Akbar's fort at Agra, or the palace at Delhi) built as a series of small porticoes (*kushk*, giving us the term *kiosk*) with one or at the most two floors, standing in a garden full of flowers and plants and enclosed by a high wall. In general, every Muslim home is divided in two parts: the *selamlek* and the *haramlek*. The first includes the rooms, spaces, and baths for men; the second is for women—the harem.

No other type of architecture makes use of such a wide variety of types and forms of arches. The rounded arch resting on columns, a Byzantine

Opposite top: The Sultan Hani caravansary, Seljuk architecture, from Turkey, thirteenth century.
Opposite center: The Registan, or Sand Plaza, Samarkand, Uzbekistan, fifteenth to eighteenth centuries.
Opposite bottom: Mausoleum of the Samanids, the beginning of a distinctly Islamic architecture, Bukhara, Uzbekistan, ca. 902.

Right: The Sultan Ahmed I Mosque, Istanbul, Ottoman architecture, 1616.
Below right: The Kaykobat madrasa, Erzurum, Turkey, Seljuk architecture, 1254.
Bottom: Patio of the Lions in the Alhambra, Granada, Spain, fourteenth century.

typology derived from the late classical period, was originally used but was eventually developed further to form complex arrangements of two superimposed arches (as in Andalusian mosques, such as that of Córdoba). The form was soon elaborated into more decorative pointed arches, used as early

as Sassanid architecture and later worked into a great number of varieties. Within a hundred years of these first versions, the Islamic arch, openly resting on columns, pilasters, or walls, had assumed a vast gamut of styles that freed it from the rigid stylistic schemes of other styles. Sometimes, in fact, different forms were grafted together or were used side by side, based on the experience of the ideas created by placing one arch atop another.

bing. Safavid domes imitated the typical covering of Mongolian and Turkish tents, accentuating the peak. The bulbous domes of India sometimes rest on airy polygonal balconies and have an emphasized pinnacle with a decorative covering, the whole recalling the shape of an upside-down floral chalice. Following the conquest of Constantinople (1453), the Ottomans elaborated a complex covering, using a large dome with a relief at its center resting on a ring supported by four large arches and flanked by a series of smaller apsidal domes and half-domes arranged along the perimeter of the structure.

The *iwan* is a large, majestic portal, typical of Iranian art, with the front supported by a large arch that in some Iranian and Indian constructions is flanked by wings on two porticoed levels. *Muqarnas* decoration appears here as the connecting element between a horizontal floor and a vertical of the building, with curved lines forming honeycombs and stalactites of a highly decorative effect. In Syria and Egypt, these were built of bare bricks, in Asia using bricks dressed with polychrome ceramics.

There is thus a long list of typologies, with schemes sometimes inspired by purely decorative concerns rather than structural demands: horseshoe arches, lanceolate arches, poly- or trilobed arches, arches raised on ribs (or on thin feet), broken arches, ladder arches, those with tiered (*muqarnas*) or zigzag decoration, and all the many kinds of pointed arches.

After the first examples of round domes in the Byzantine or Sassanid style, the first distinctively Islamic domes were created in Egypt, where they were narrowed, set upon a high ring (the drum), and connected to the square supporting structure by means of angular chamfers. Many types of connecting structures (funnel-shaped, pendentive, bowed, niched, bowl-shaped, *muqarnas*) were later applied to domes. The Turkomans covered their domes with a conical roof, while Mongol domes are typically bulbous and set on very high drums, often with bean-shaped decoration or rib-

The mosque (from the Arabic *masjid*, "place for prostration") is the place of worship in which the Muslim community unites, especially for ritual prayers on Fridays at noon. Thus it is a large hall. The characteristic element of every place of prayer is the mihrab, a large niche—a sort of large altar at times splendidly decorated—in the direction of the Ka'ba, thus indicating the direction to face in prayer. Beside the mihrab is often a minbar, a sort of pulpit of marble, brick, or wood, traditionally composed of a richly decorated flight of stairs with a platform. A mosque also has areas for ablutions and a library open to the faithful.

Somewhat similar to the mosque is the madrasa,

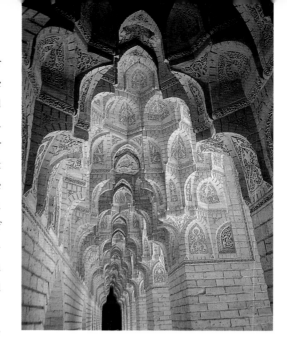

Opposite top: Dome of the mosque of Ghom, Iran, seventeenth century.
Opposite center: Dome of the mausoleum of Jalal al-Din Rumi, Konya, Turkey.
Opposite bottom: Dome of the Hall of the Two Sisters, Alhambra, Granada, Spain, fourteenth century.
Above: Vault with *muqarnas* decoration in the Dair al-Dur mosque, Iraq, twelfth century.
Left: Dome of the Grand Mosque of Córdoba.
Below: Portal with *muqarnas* decoration, Gok madrasa, Sivas, Turkey, 1271.

the educational institution. These first came into being in Iraq and Khorasan at the instigation of the minister Nizam al-Mulk at the end of the eleventh century; the structure of most madrasas follows that typical of Iranian universities. Under the Ottomans, the madrasa was expanded into a vast assembly of buildings called the *kulliyye*: the mosque, various teaching faculties, a hospital, public library, dormitory, and dining hall. Large *kulliyye* were founded by Beyazid II at Amasya and Edirne and by Mehmet II and Sulayman I at Istanbul.

The Minaret

The mosque, the sacred building of Islam, has a well-defined structure, with certain necessary areas, decorations, and ornaments. The minaret (from *manara*, "lighthouse"; also *sawma'a, mi'dhana*), which towers over the mosque and from which the muezzin calls (*adhan*) the faithful to prayer, while common, is not among the established elements. In the opinion of certain scholars, the origins of the minaret lead back to the sepulchral towers of Palmyra, to Egyptian obelisks, and to the *massebah* (commemorative funerary stela used by the peoples known as Semitic); there are also those who trace them back to Christian bell towers, but this seems less likely, since minarets appeared first.

The first minaret was built at Basra in 665 by Ziyad ibn Abit. At first, minarets were constructed within the walls of the mosque courtyard, most often at the center of the northern side, and had square bases, sometimes with a round second floor and a third shaped like a hexagonal chapel. Two spiral minarets were famous during the early ninth century, that of the mosque of Samarra (160 feet high) and the Abu Dulaf mosque in Iraq.

With the Seljuks (eleventh century), the cylindrical minaret appeared, usually with ceramic dec-

Above: Square minaret, mosque of Hasan, Rabat, Morocco, 1195.

Left: Organ-pipe minaret, Cifte Minare madrasa, Sivas, Turkey, 1272.

Right: Spiral minaret, Samarra, Iraq, ninth century.

Below: Needle minaret, Sultan Ahmet I Mosque, Istanbul, 1616.

Bottom: Organ-pipe minaret, Allikuli of Khiva, Uzbekistan, 1812.

ferent types of minarets, the organ-pipe (central Asia) and the needle (Turkey). With the Moguls in India and the Ottomans in their vast empire, minarets grew to four, located on the corners of the building or in the space on which the mosque itself stood; in rare cases a single mosque might have six minarets.

The Mameluke style of Egypt, later applied throughout North Africa and in Andalusia, used a single minaret, often isolated and located to the right side of the building, always thin, with a square base and a final crowning section.

oration; the shape of the top varied, but was usually conical in Turkey and like a canopy in Iran. At first only one minaret, standing alone, was used; then two appeared, located to the side of the large main portal, called the *iwan*, or at the monumental entry to the building. There were then two dif

Islamic Ceramics

Islamic art has a very long history, with many schools and styles. Within the many forms of art, ceramics present a distinctly Islamic expression, one that is important from several points of view. Until the advent of Islam, the Western world used only two glazes, and the many colors and beautiful glazes of ancient Egyptian and Mesopotamian wares had been forgotten for centuries. Then a style of ceramics appeared during the Abbasid period (750–1258) that was based on the art of glazes from the steppe region of central Asia, land of the barbaric Turkish

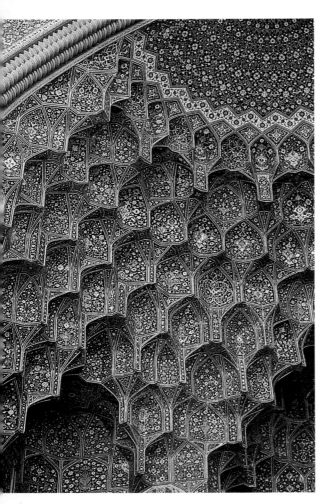

and Mongolian populations that also brought the enameling of metal (*cloisonné* and *champlevé*) to China and Europe. In the cities of Samarra and Baghdad, the Turkish masters applied these enamel techniques to ceramics, developing not just applied barbotine slips with molded relief decoration, but also tin-glazed decoration in white, blue, yellow, green, and purple, and lead glazes that repeated the characteristic Chinese "three colors" (*t'o tai*), with sgraffito decoration applied to the unbaked clay.

During the period of Harun al-Rashid (caliph from 786 to 809), alchemists created innovative materials and techniques, including the use of various metallic salts on all types of glazes, thus creating lusterware, pottery with an iridescent metallic sheen, used on white, polychrome, or monochrome glazes. This type of pottery was thus a truly Islamic creation. An excellent example is the decoration of the mihrab of the Okba mosque (862) at Kairouan, Tunisia. The most important treatise of the time on the various techniques was written by the Iranian Abu al-Qasim, inventor of *rang-e do ateshi*: twice-fired colors, meaning ceramics fired at a high heat, painted again, and then fired at a lower heat.

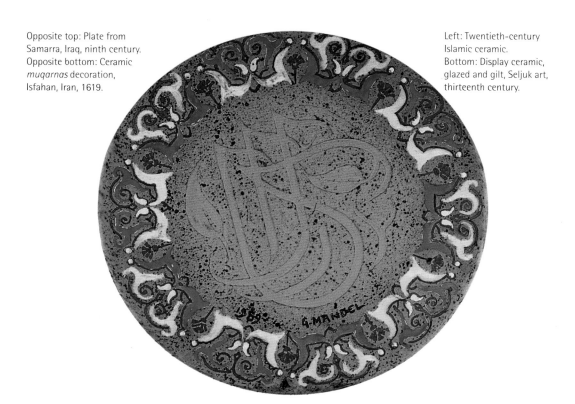

Opposite top: Plate from Samarra, Iraq, ninth century.
Opposite bottom: Ceramic *muqarnas* decoration, Isfahan, Iran, 1619.

Left: Twentieth-century Islamic ceramic.
Bottom: Display ceramic, glazed and gilt, Seljuk art, thirteenth century.

During the Persian Samanid dynasty (819–1005), truly Islamic art can be said to have come into being, meaning art that was no longer related to late antiquity but was a new style created from the union of steppe and classical forms. Two techniques were used, slip and glaze (purple, green, red, yellow, brown), with the outstanding examples being made at Samarkand (Afrasiyab), Nishapur (polychrome ceramics on a white ground), Sari, and Gurgan.

Lusterware and sgraffito decoration were well developed during the Fatimid dynasty in Egypt, Syria, and North Africa (930–1021), but the period also saw the large-scale migration of ceramic masters to every region of the Islamic world. During the Abbasid period, the technique of polychrome lead glazes was further perfected.

The arrival of the Seljuk Turks—who entered Baghdad in 1055—gave an enormous impulse to ceramic art. The application of the style of covering tents in polychrome felt to architectural constructions led to the great decorations using *kashi* tiles and mosaics. Tableware were decorated with sgraffito (Amol), with *champlevé* (Gabri and Garrus), or in *cloisonné* (Aghkand, Syria), with piercing or

silhouettes (black glaze decorated in sgraffito and covered by transparent alkaline green glaze, typical of Gurgan and Rayy); using the classic lusterware; with the *minai* technique (so-called *halt-rangi* enamels; seven colors); or with the beautiful *lajvardina* technique with lapis lazuli and coloring added after the third firing over glaze. Finally there was the highly complicated style of *lakabi*, painting in several layers (Rakka). Household crockery came into common use during this period, its body made using a kind of frit mixture (ten parts quartz, one white clay, one baked glass), creating a hard, thin covering that may have been in imitation of

Chinese porcelain. In fact, the white porcelain of the Chinese T'ang period was much imitated.

These techniques were inherited by the Mongol Ilkhanids (1256–1336) and the Iranian Timurids (1387–1502). Farther to the west, the Mameluke rulers of Egypt (1250–1517) experimented with these techniques and exported to Europe beautiful apothecary jars (*albarelli*) painted under luster glazes with sgraffito decoration or in imitation of blue-and-white Chinese ceramics. Muslim Spain (the Umayyad and Nasrid dynasties, 756–1492) preferred lead glazes and the technique called *cuerda seca*. The principal centers of ceramic production in Spain were Maiorca (source of majolica), Manises, Valencia, and Paterna. Catholic Spain carried on these techniques in the ceramic style called Hispano-Moresque.

Particular ceramics were made in Iran during the Safavid (1502–1736) and Kajar (1796–1925) periods. Most common were ceramics made using the *kubachi* technique, with black underglaze painting; imitations of Chinese blue-and-white; blue and black or polychrome colors under transparent glazes; a late style of lusterware; and the Kirman technique in both mono- and polychrome.

MUHAMMAD SEEN FROM THE WEST

The conquest of much of the ancient world, the occupation of the southern end of the Mediterranean Sea, the arrival of Muslims in Spain and Sicily, the fall of Constantinople, and finally the Turks outside the walls of Vienna made Muhammad Europe's most dangerous enemy, a role in which he was cast

The last great movement in Islamic ceramics took place under the Ottomans, who in their vast empire distributed splendid polychrome ceramics, first in the Iznik style and later in the Kutahia, along with the popular Chanakkale ceramics, which were also made in imitations of European styles but of a refinement and technical execution of great quality.

Opposite top: *Minai* cup from Kashan, thirteenth century.
Opposite bottom: Ceramic mihrab with alkaline glaze, Iran, 1354, Metropolitan Museum of Art, New York.
Above: Plate from Iznik, Turkey, sixteenth century.
Right: Muhammad enthroned, fifteenth-century miniature from the *Decameron* by Giovanni Boccaccio.
Below: Ceramic panel from the Alhambra of Granada, thirteenth century.

for a long time. An almost constant campaign of disinformation concerning Muhammad in the West contributed to creating divisions and hatreds whose echoes can still be heard.

Word of the Prophet first reached Europe by way of Byzantium and the Mozarabic Christians living in Muslim Spain. Among the first authors to mention him were John of Damascus (ca. 675–749) in his summary of heresies, *De Haeresibus Liber*, and the ninth-century Anastasius the Librarian in

Other works that defamed the Prophet include *Li livres dou tresor*—the first vernacular encyclopedia—by Brunetto Latini (1268) and the *Golden Legend*, the collection of saints' lives by Jacobus da Varagine (1280). In the *Libre del gentil e los tres savis* (1267) by Raymond Lully, a Jew, Christian, and Muslim present competing eulogies of their respective faiths. In England, the defamation of Muhammad began in 1362 with *Piers Plowman* by William Langland and a reference by John Lydate in his *Falls of Princes* (1483).

John Mandeville (1300–1371) made use of much of this information in his *Voyages*, the denigrating aspects of which were later repeated by the German Dominican monk Ricoldus (d. 1320) in his *Confutatio Alcorani*, a work praised by Martin Luther.

More balanced views of Muhammad began appearing in the eighteenth century, for example in the *Life of Muhammad* by Henri de Boulainvilliers, which was published in London in 1730; the

his *Chronographia*, based on the work by Theophanes. Important references to Muhammad also came from the Spaniard Eulogio de Córdoba (ninth century) and Pedro de Alfonso in his *Dialogues* (eleventh–twelfth centuries). The early eleventh-century treatise *Epistola Saraceni* was of a certain importance, serving as the source for such libelous works as the *Speculum Historiale* by Vincent of Beauvais and the *Quadruplex Reprobatio* by an anonymous author. All of these texts presented Muhammad as a kind of magician, lustful and ignorant, ferocious and bloodthirsty, most of all schismatic. The notoriety of the Prophet in Europe led to various historical legends, and there are references to Muhammad in the *Chanson de Roland* (ca. 1100), the *Cycle of Guillaume d'Orange*, and the *Historia Orientalis* by Jacques de Vitry (ca. 1219).

Alphonse de Lamartine

"Never did man propose to himself, voluntarily or otherwise, an end more sublime, since this end was superhuman; to sap the superstitions interposed between the creature and the Creator, to bring back God to man and man to God, to restore the rational and the holy idea of the Divinity amid that chaos of the material and disfigured deities of idolatry. Never did man undertake with resources so feeble a task so disproportioned to human forces ... If the grandeur of the design, the pettiness of the means, the immensity of the result be the three measures of human genius, who could dare to compare humanly the greatest men of modern times to Muhammad? ... What man was greater by all the scales on which we measure human greatness?"

Alphonse de Lamartine (1790-1869),
Histoire de la Turquie

text was soon attacked by Jean Ganier in his own *Vie de Mahomet* (1732), which emphasized the negative aspects of the "schismatic."

During the eighteenth century Muhammad became the hero of literary works, in particular theatrical compositions, outstanding of which was the tragedy by Voltaire (*Le Fanatisme de Mahomet le Prophète*), staged in Paris in 1742 but censured by the local clergy. It was reprised in a different form by Henry Brooke in 1778. Goethe wrote a poem about Muhammad, "Mahomets Gesang" (The Song of Muhammad) in 1773.

In the nineteenth century the historical reality of the man was finally accepted, as in the poem "Mahomets Traum in de Wüste" (1804) and the drama *Mahomet oder der Prohet von Mekka* (1805), both by Karoline von Günderode. Muhammad

also appears in three long sections of Victor Hugo's long poem "La Légende des Siècles" (1859).

These are only a few of the major voices in European literature, which from the seventh century to today has offered such an abundance of

refutations, confutations, acrimonious assaults, and denigrations that, in the end, they must be seen as a reflection of the great importance of the Prophet even outside the Islamic world. The situation has not been helped by collateral subjects. As the French historian Daniel Roux wrote, from the sixteenth century to the last century, "the libels written against the Ottoman Empire were more numerous than those written about the United States of America."

Alongside attacks, there was also much interest in the Koran. The first edition in Latin—actually a tendentious "paraphrasing"—was made in 1143 by Peter the Venerable, abbot of Cluny (manuscript in the Arsenal Library, Paris). It was later printed by Theodor Bibliander (Buchmann) at Basel in 1543 and

Below: Page from one of the first Arabic–Latin dictionaries, Rome, 1786.

Above: Alfonso X the Wise, the Spanish king considered a friend of the Muslims.

at Zurich in 1550, with a preface by Martin Luther.

These various translations served as the basis of the first Italian translation, by Andrea Arrivabene, published at Venice in 1547. Arrivabene's work was used as the basis for the first German version, by H. Salomon Schweigger (Nuremberg, 1616), which in turn was the basis for the first Dutch edition, by an anonymous author (Hamburg, 1641). The first French translation, by André de Ryer (Paris, 1647), served as the basis for the first English edition, by Alexander Ross (London, 1648 or 1649), which defined Muhammad as the Antichrist.

There is then the noteworthy second Latin version, with facing text, by Ludovico Maracci (Padua, 1698), revised by Reinuccio in 1721. It gives the impression that Latin is the best language for achieving a version close to the original not just in terms of concept but also rhythm and spirit.

Today there are about 600 versions of the Koran in forty-six languages. The lion's share is in English, with 166 editions, followed by French with seventy-eight and German with seventy-five.

Dante and Muhammad

Versions of the story of the Prophet's journey to heaven (the mir'aj) were popular during the Middle Ages, leading during the second half of the thirteenth century to the Escala de Mahoma, Eschiele Mahomet, and Scalo Mahomete, on which Dante Alighieri drew for his Divine Comedy, in which Muhammad and Ali are located in the Inferno (Canto XXVIII: 25–36), among the creators of schisms, in the eighth circle, ninth bolgia:

His entrails were hanging between his legs,
and the vitals could be seen and the foul sack
that makes ordure of what is swallowed.

While I was all absorbed in gazing on him,
he looked at me and with his hands pulled open his
breast, saying, "Now see how I rend myself!

"See how mangled is Muhammad!
In front of me goes Ali weeping,
cleft in the face from chin to forelock.

"And all the others whom you see here
were in their lifetime sowers of scandal and schism,
and therefore are thus cleft."

Two precious miniatures from an antique codex of the Divine Comedy by Dante, fourteenth century, Gerolamini Library, Naples. Recent studies indicate that the first two cantos of this codex may have once belonged to the poet himself, who made several corrections on them in his own hand.

An Aspect of Islam: Fundamentalism

Much has been said about fundamentalism, and it certainly is not an unimportant topic, for which reason we must address it, however briefly. The French author and politician Roger Garaudy puts it this way: "Fundamentalism, all fundamentalisms, whether technocratic, Stalinist, Christian, Jewish, or Islamic, constitute today the greatest danger for the future. At a time when the only choice we have

is between mutual destruction and dialogue, their victories ghettoize the entire human community into fanatical sects closed in on themselves and therefore eager for confrontation. . . . Fundamentalism is the greatest danger for our epoch, an epoch in which no problem can be resolved on the basis of a single community and its dogmas. In effect, fundamentalism, every fundamentalism, is the diseased side of all humanity, it is the crazed cells, the malignant tumor."

Bearing in mind that fundamentalism is a political manifestation or a paranoid sect of a form of power that merely "borrows" a religious appearance, Islamic fundamentalism, in the words of Roberto Guiducci, "is often the only response possible to colonialism in progress." There is territorial colonialism, political colonialism, and economic colonialism; with so many forms of colonialism, is it any wonder there are so many forms of fundamentalism?

Within this vast sphere, the world of Islam can be divided into eight territorial divisions, each with its own type of political fundamentalism. The first group is composed of Egypt, Syria, Iraq, and Yemen, in which the confrontation between state capitalism and agrarian reform has led to the creation of bureaucratic machinery that excludes the independent middle class. It should be noted that this group, and others like it, was originally supported by the Communist party, a party that in and of itself is in opposition to the concept of Islam.

The second group includes Algeria, Tunisia, and Libya, states that are ruled by military leaders who have entrusted reform to a small private sector with results that are more political than economic.

The states in the third group—Indonesia, Pakistan, and Bangladesh—are still in the process of integrating the system of rule by wealthy families and large landowners.

The fourth group is composed of Saudi

Opposite: The outer wall (*bottom*) and great central hall (*top*) of the asylum of Edirne, Turkey, built by Beyazid II between 1488 and 1498. During that period of the Ottoman Empire, many of the people enclosed in the asylum were fanatics and fundamentalists, at the time considered to be simply mental deviants.

Entry to the mausoleum (*above*) and the interior (*left*) with the cenotaph of the great Sufi master and poet Al-Hallaj (857–922), who was executed by fundamentalists at Baghdad.

Arabia, Brunei, the United Arab Emirates, Kuwait, Oman, and Bahrain, states that exclude every form of democracy, all political dialogue, all economic independence. In Saudi Arabia the economy and most of all the lucrative oil sector are the exclusive domain of the 6,000 members of the royal family. All opposition, such as that of Katif in 1948 or that of Muhammad al-Qahtani in 1979, is violently suppressed.

The fifth group is composed of Jordan and Morocco, in which liberal royal power is flanked by a democracy capable of making its voice heard.

The sixth group is composed of Afghanistan, Sudan, and Nigeria, in which sectarian, tribal, and religious divisions weaken the process of integration, leading to explosive forms of protest. Afghanistan is currently in a state of transition between a past that is only too recent and an unforeseeable future.

Iran would seem to present a separate case. Its

wealth has drawn the interest of France, Britain, and the United States, which have taken up positions of propaganda in their efforts to carry on an economic colonialism that should be the subject of what is said about Iran in the West and should also be the object of opposition in Iran. The shah

was driven out by the people, unwilling to put up with his despotism, but then put back in power in 1953 thanks to a coup organized by the CIA; the shah then sent thousands of businessmen into exile or prison in 1975. The waste of 40 percent of the nation's earnings on armaments, the shah's nepotism, and the favor he showed his armed forces completely alienated him from any possible favor of the people. That led to a popular revolution, following which it was very easy for France to support the ayatollah Ruhollah Khomeini.

failure of their economic and developmental policies; because of the continuous derision heaped on Islamic thinking and lifestyle; because of the policies of Western powers that seek to weaken Islamic positions in Muslim countries, demonizing Islamic leaders, supporting oppressive regimes if they are friendly to the West, and reducing Muslim states to economically indigent societies full of debts."

We can only conclude that no "real" fundamentalism exists within the Islamic "religion," or within the monotheistic religions in general, since

Opposite top: The crowd praying at Teheran on the tenth anniversary of the death of the imam Khomeini.

Opposite bottom: Women of Kabul, Afghanistan, in front of a hospital.

Right: Uzbek Muslim women going to prayers being held in a fabric factory because of the prohibitions imposed by the local government.

Only one country with a Muslim majority presents itself as a model of tolerant Islam: Turkey. The Turkic regions that still suffer the bloody oppression of Russia look to Turkey: Chechnya, Azerbaijan, Turkestan, Turkmenistan, and so on to Chinese Turkestan.

According to two leading scholars, Ziauddin Sardar and Zafar Abbas Malik, "Islamic fundamentalism has been taking hold because of the excesses of several modernist leaders; because of the

the problem is not an excess of religion but rather a lack of it. Every religion points the way toward the good, toward mysticism, toward enlightenment, but—and it is the reverse of the same coin— every religion can lead to fundamentalism, fanaticism, terrorism. Fanatics and terrorists are what religions become when they mix, adding in more or less virulence, these four ingredients: presumption, ignorance, hypocrisy, and paranoia, none of which is a quality exclusive to Islam.

in Islam

"Man or woman, every Muslim must study." The Turkish emperor Ulug-Beg (1393–1449) had that saying of the Prophet Muhammad engraved on the facade of the universities he founded in Bukhara and Samarkand. Those universities were attended by both men and women, many of the women going on to distinguish themselves as judges and teachers. That was anything but rare in the Islamic world during the golden period. Today, throughout the world, there seem to be no more such golden days. Even so, the swirl of ethnic and cultural realities. The Koran freed women from pre-Islamic mistreatment, giving them legal rights, protecting their property and their right to inherit, entrusting children to them in case of divorce; and in the case of divorce, which either the man or the woman can request, Koranic law provides

that the woman keep all her property, all gifts she has received, and one quarter of her husband's property. Under Islam, the woman can choose to abort if she wishes, and only the woman can make that decision, not the man. There are thus good reasons why Si Hamza Boubakeur, one of the leading theologians of this century, wrote in his *Modern Treatise of Islamic Theology* (Paris, 1985): "Poorly informed people and the detractors of Islam, who in general do not back away from any lie, accuse Islam of having destroyed the female condition. However, no known religion, whether pagan or revealed, monotheistic or polytheistic, is as favorable to children and to women as Islam."

In Islam, marriage is a social contract, not a

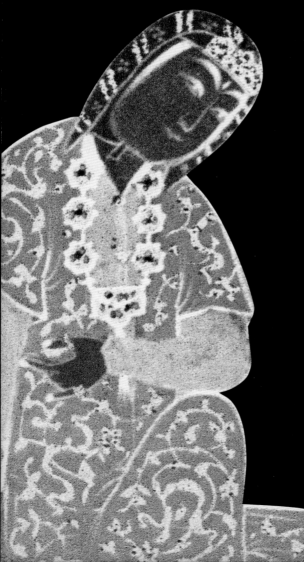

sacrament. In the Koran the rules of marriage—and women's rights of inheritance—are quite clear, expressed in the second sura, from verse 221 to verse 242. The woman is socially protected by numerous verses in the fourth sura. It is of course true that in certain backward Islamic countries, in places where pre-Islamic customs and habits survive, the prescriptions of the Koran are not always fully followed.

As for the veil, it is not a specific Koranic obligation (the Koran promotes modesty and suitable clothing). The veil is a pre-Islamic custom, still sometimes encountered in non-Muslim communities. In regular use in some countries, it is not even accepted in certain others. In the same country there can be areas in which the veil is worn and areas in which it is not.

We can now briefly review the role of the Muslim woman in history, beginning with Sufi women. The volume *Sufi Women* by Sheikh Javad Nurbakhsh, leader of the Iranian confraternity of the Nimatalla Sufi, cites 124. Of particular importance was the Turk Fatima al-Nisaburiyya, spiritual master of Dhu al-Nun al-Misri. Many Muslim women have been queens, state leaders, or warriors. Perhaps the most important was Raziya Sultan, thirteenth-century sultan of Delhi. In 1232 she conquered the state of Gwalior. In her book *Turkish Women as Sovereigns and Regents of Islamic States,* the late writer Bahriye Üçok, deputy to the Turkish government, lists sixteen non-Turkish queens and twenty-eight rulers of Turkish states, including queens, empresses, and regents. Among these are Shajar al-Durr, the Mameluke queen of Egypt from 1249 to 1250, and the dynasty of the Begum, who reigned in the Indian state of Bhopal from 1844 to 1926. The last was the Begum Sultan Jahan, who reigned from 1901 to 1926. Some *valide* sultans (mothers of reigning sultans) of the Turkish Ottoman court were regents on the imperial throne during the minority of their sons. Some Islamic states today have female ministers.

Opposite: The shah of Iran visits Raziya Sultan of Delhi, miniature from *Famous Queens*, 1428. Below: Haseki Sultan, Ottoman queen mother, miniature from the eighteenth century. Above: Fatima Sultan, queen of the Kasim khanate, ceramic from ca. 1810.

And Tomorrow, Which Islam?

With colonialism, the glories of Islamic civilization were forgotten or suffocated. Science became magic, religion became superstition. In the period following World War II, the colonized Muslim peoples succeeded in freeing themselves from the yoke of foreigners, although they were unable to free themselves completely from Western exploitation. Thus began the difficult process of reviving ancient identities, reattaching societies to roots that had not always remained alive, reject-

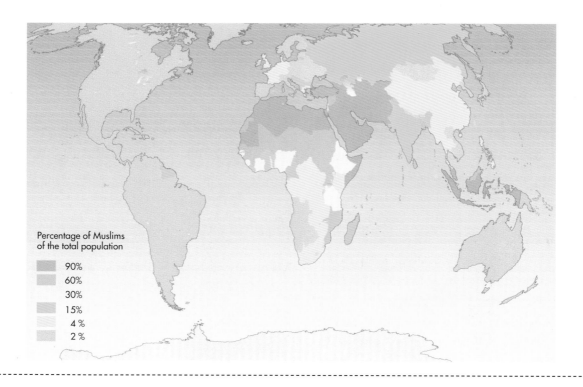

ing whatever of the West had taken hold during the colonial period, and becoming increasingly convinced that Islam should not make a servile entry to the realm of the dollar or the ruble but should instead regain its own identity. The process of decolonization was long. Syria became free of the League of Nations mandate in 1945, Jordan in 1946; Pakistan won independence in 1947, Indonesia in 1949. These last two Muslim states are among the most populous, with 200 million inhabitants together.

Between 1955 and 1965, the last Muslim states of Africa gained independence. The Turkic states annexed to Russia, to which can be added Chinese Turkestan, represent a large group that has still not achieved independence. These regions amount to about 50 million

Above: Modern version of *Basmala*.
Below: The Muslim population of the world.

Opposite top: Poster of the imam Khomeini at Isfahan.
Opposite bottom: Kemal Atatürk.

Percentage of Muslims of the total population

- 90%
- 60%
- 30%
- 15%
- 4%
- 2%

Muslims that officially have only three hundred mosques, a thousand *ulama*, two Koranic universities, and a single quarterly periodical. The researchers Alexandre Benningsen and Chantal Lemercier-Quelquejay calculate that "within twenty years at the most, one of three former Soviet citizens will be Muslim."

Catholicism has a central organization, with vast power and centuries of proven experience, as well as a leader endowed with full governing power. Islam has none of that, therefore no one has the power to remove or modify a single verse of the Koran, a ritual, or a holiday. The most important Islamic organizations have no general authority. Among the numerous organizations is the World Muslim League, created at Mecca in 1962, and the Muslim Conference (a conference of the foreign ministers of Islamic states), created at Jidda in 1970. The many periodicals on Islamic life and many new Islamic cultural centers in the West are clear signs of Islamic ferment and European interest in Islam.

Among the cultural centers is the Institut für Geshichte der Arabish-Islamischen Wissenschaften of Frankfurt, the American Islamic College of Chicago, and the Islamic Academy of Cambridge. Also

who belongs to the Jerrahi-Halveti Sufi *tariqa*.

Before converting to Islam, Roger Garaudy, French deputy, president of the National Assembly, and founder of the center for Marxist studies, was a fervent Communist. During that period of his life he wrote *God Is Dead*. In 1947 he founded and directed the International Institute for the Dialogue of Civilizations in Córdoba, Spain.

A potential dialogue between Islam and the Catholic church began with Father Henri Laurman (1862–1937), Miguel Asin y Palacios (1871–1944), and Louis Massignon (1883–1962): their individual efforts may have contributed to the spirit of the Vatican Council II. The council's declaration *Nostra Aetate* (No. 3) says: "The Church regards with esteem also the Muslims. They adore the one

important are the many collections of Islamic art, some of notable size, many of which are in French and British museums. Such collections provide valuable insight into the essential values of Muslim civilization. Behind this cultural fervor is another phenomena, the increase in conversions, a noteworthy fact particularly since Islam has no missionaries and does not support religious propaganda. Many famous people in the West have converted to Islam. Among the best known are the choreographer Maurice Béjart; the British singer Cat Stevens (Yusuf Islam); the illustrious scholar of Sufism and director of Éditions du Seuil of Paris, Michel Chodkiewicz; the eminent writer and Sufi Eva de Vitray Meyerovic; the oceanographer Jacques Cousteau; and the singer Franco Battiato,

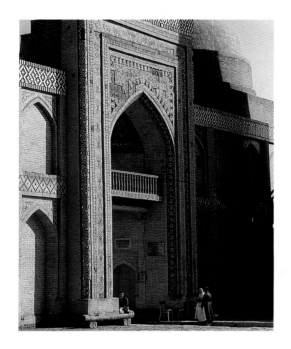

formed by Sufi confraternities, which by now are widespread throughout the world. Among the most active are the Naqshibandiyya, the Qadiriyya, and the Jerrahiyya-Khalwatiyya. Without doubt, given the continuous desire for renewed and profound spirituality now appearing in a West troubled by materialism and consumerism, Islam presents a luminous and authentic model. Preached by the Prophet Muhammad fourteen hundred years ago, it is still powerfully vital today as it heads into the coming future.

Opposite top: The entry to the venerable mosque of Karbala, Iraq.
Opposite bottom: The modern mosque of Turfan in Chinese Turkestan.

Left: One of the portals of the Qadiriyya retreat, Baghdad.
Below: The Ottoman sultan Selim III in a portrait by Hippolyte Berteaux (1843–1926).

God, living and subsisting in himself, merciful and all-powerful, the creator of heaven and earth, who has spoken to men." From 1964 to 1974 an Office for Islam was active, later becoming the Commission for Islam. The Ecumenical Council of Churches has a commission called Dialogue with the Religions and Ideologies of Our Time (DRI).

In the West there are the notable works per-

Johann Wolfgang Goethe

"An entire race lifts its prince on high! In rolling triumph, it gives names to the lands and cities that grow along its path. Irresistibly, it rushes onward, leaving behind a wake of flame-tipped towers and marble palaces, creations of its vigor. Like Atlas, it bears cedar houses upon its giant shoulders; over its head the wind loudly flaps a thousand flags as testimony to its glory. And so, bursting with joy, it brings its brothers, its treasures, its children into the waiting bosom of its Father."

Johann Wolfgang Goethe (1749-1832),
"Mahomets Gesang"

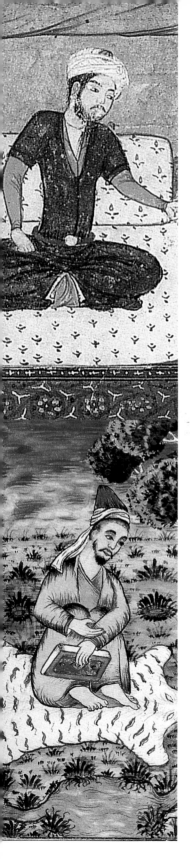

Sayings of the Prophet

If anyone of you leads the people in prayer, he should shorten it, for among them are the weak, the sick, the old; and if anyone among you prays alone, then he may prolong the prayer as much as he wishes.

Bukhari, X:62

Whoever has the following four characteristics will be a pure hypocrite, and whoever has one of the following four characteristics will have one characteristic of hypocrisy unless and until he gives it up: When he is entrusted, he betrays. Whenever he speaks, he tells a lie. Whenever he makes a covenant, he proves treacherous. Whenever he quarrels, he behaves in a very imprudent, evil, and insulting manner.

Bukhari, II:24

Three signs reveal the hypocrite: when he talks, he lies; when he makes a promise, he does not keep it; when he is loaned something, he does not return it.

Bukhari, LXXVIII:49 (2)

When every security has disappeared, expect to see the End of the World. When authority is in the hands of those who are not worthy, expect to see the arrival of the End of the World.

Bukhari, III:2

Do not speak ill of the dead; they have arrived at the place they merited.

Bukhari, XXIII:97

Which alms will be those most largely repaid? The alms given by the healthy and greedy man who fears poverty and desires wealth.

Bukhari, XXIV:11 (2)

Money received in alms is beautiful and pleasing. He who receives it without greed will find fortune; but he who takes it greedily will be unable to profit thereby. It will be to him like food to one who eats without satiety. The hand that gives is worth more than the hand that receives.

Bukhari, XXIV:5 (4)

The poor man is not the man who must be content with only one or two mouthfuls of food; the truly poor man is he who, having nothing, is ashamed to ask or does not know how to ask people with the necessary insistence.

Bukhari, XXIV:53 (1)

There are three things of which God disapproves: cunning plans, the waste of goods, and excessive requests. And three are the enemies of my religion: the fundamentalist, the fundamentalist, the fundamentalist.

Bukhari, XXIV:53 (2)

He who is of a marriageable age should get married; marriage is the best way to extinguish lascivious looks and to control carnal desires. He that cannot marry should fast; doing so will calm him.

Bukhari, XXX:10

Going along a road a man sensed a strong thirst and went into a well to drink. When he came out he saw a dog that, suffering thirst, was panting and licking the ground. "This animal is suffering as much thirst as I did," he thought and returned to the well to fill his boot with water. He climbed up again and gave the dog water to drink. God was pleased by his gesture and pardoned his sins. Thus, when you ask me, "Will we be repaid for the good we do to our animals?" My response is that there will be recompense for everyone who gives to drink to any being that has a beating heart.

Bukhari, XLII:9 (1)

He that becomes a slave to money, to luxurious clothes, to sumptuous gowns, who is happy when he receives and is in pain when he does not receive, will go to ruin.

Bukhari, LVI:70 (2)

It can happen that a man will seem to have the behavior of the elect while instead he will be among the damned; it can happen that a man will seem to be among the damned while instead he will be one of the elect.

Bukhari, LVI:77

War is a deceptive error.

Bukhari, LVI:157 (3)

Dot not trust in suspicions, because a suspicion can be more dishonest than reality. Do not be indiscreet, do not spy, do not be envious, do not hate, do not get angry. Be brothers, for you are the servants of God.

Bukhari, LXXVIII:58

The energetic man is not one who uses force but one who keeps control of himself in a moment of anger.

Bukhari, LXVIII:76 (1)

If he had two valleys full of wealth, the son of Adam would want a third; only the tomb satisfies the belly of the son of Adam. However, some of them turn instead to God.

Bukhari, LXXX:10 (2)

Wealth does not consist in abundance of goods; wealth is wealth of the soul.

Bukhari, LXXXI:15

When one of you looks upon someone more favored in wealth and beauty, he should look also on those who are less favored than him.

Bukhari, LXXXI:30

The attentive man keeps his coveting under control and acts on the basis of what will happen after his death. Negligent instead is he who abandons his soul to his lustful instincts and has vain dreams of God.

Tirmidhi, Nawwawi, I:5 (7)

Do not overlook the performance of a good work, even if it is simply meeting a brother with a serene face.

Muslim, Nawwawi, I:13 (5)

He that invites others to follow the right way will be repaid just as those who follow it; and that in no sense diminishes the repayment. He that invites others to follow the wrong road will be punished just as he that follows it, and that in no sense diminishes the punishment.

Muslim, Nawwawi, I:20 (2)

Renounce this world and God will love you; renounce the possessions of other people and the people will love you.

Ibn Maja, Nawwawi, I:55 (16)

The son of Adam has the right to possess only four things: a home in which to rest, clothes to cover himself, a portion of bread, a portion of water.

Tirmidhi, Nawwawi, I:55 (26)

The son of Adam keeps invoking, "My goods, my goods." But in reality what do you ever possess, O son of Adam, beyond what you have eaten, what you have worn and worn out, what you have given in alms, and what you have brought to a good conclusion?

Muslim, Nawwasi, I:55 (27)

Glossary

A

- ablution: *see* wudu
- abrar: the pure, the good; a grade of the hierarchy of the "Friends" of God.
- akhira: the future life, the afterlife.
- alam: the world, the cosmos, the whole of created things. Fifty-eight species of worlds exist, including *alam al-Malakut*, the celestial kingdom of God; *alam al-Jabarut*, the world of divine omnipotence; *alam al-Nasut*, the world of the human senses; and *alam al-Shahada*, the world of the sensible manifestation.
- al-Asma al-Husna: the "most beautiful names," the ninety-nine names attributed to God and indicated by the Koran that constitute the ninety-nine beads (or thirty-three, to repeat three times) of the *tashbi* rosary. These are divided into names of essences and names of qualities.
- Allah: God. Contraction of the definite article *al* and *ilah*, divinity. In the pre-Islamic period and in particular in the kingdoms of southern Arabia, the divinity was already called Allah: *allah* in the masculine and *allaha (al-Lat)* in the feminine; and there was a god called by that name. It appears in the form *HLH* in Lihyanite inscriptions of the fifth century BC, in a Minean inscription discovered at Ula, and in others Nabatean. It is found in the form *Hallah* in an inscription of Safa from the first century AD and in a Christian inscription at Umm al-Jimal (Syria) of the sixth century AD. It was probably introduced to Syria from the Arabian Peninsula, but in any case it appears as a Meccan divinity in the pagan period among the tribal divinities of the Quraysh. The father of the Prophet Muhammad was named Abdullah. With the preaching of the Prophet the term *Allah* lost the character of being the name of a god to become instead the word for the generalized indication of absolute divinity, with the specific idea of his singularity and oneness. Such is the nominative form that is expressed in the formulaic declaration of faith called the *Shahada* (*La Ilaha illa Allah:* "No other god but God").
- Ansar: helper. Name given the people of Medina who welcomed and helped the Prophet.
- aqila: important institution in Islamic penal law based on tribal origins according to which the entire family of a murderer, or all his relatives, or all his associates, are held accountable for the murder committed.
- aqiqa: ritual sacrifice performed seven days after the birth of a son, who is given his name on that same day. The sacrifice can be performed later, even by the son in adult life. Most of the meat is distributed among the poor.
- arabesque: term used in the West for the typical decorative elements of Islamic art. Among the various forms are vegetal, geometric, and calligraphic.
- arkan: column, element. There are Five Pillars of Islam, three obligatory *(Shahada; salat;*

zakat) and two optional (the fast in the month of Ramadan and the pilgrimage to Mecca).
- asabiyya: the "spirit of relationship from consanguinity" that united the Arabs before Islam and that the Prophet replaced in the name of the "relationship through the religion of Islam."
- ashura: name of the tenth day of the month of Muharram, day of expiation and of fasting (optional), established by the Prophet in imitation of the Hebrew asur when he arrived at Medina.
- aya (plural *ayat*): sign, verse (in particular the verses of the Koran), parable, testimony; the miraculous signs of nature that God has distributed on the earth so humans can learn to read them.

B

- banun: the sons (*banu* in combining form: "the sons of"). Singular *ibn* (if used at the beginning; *ben* is in the middle).
- baraka: blessing, spiritual influence.
- basmala: the formula *Bismi Llahi al-Rahmani al-rahimi*—"In the name of God, the compassionate, the merciful"—that begins every sura in the Koran except for the ninth; also begins every action of every good Muslim. It is also called *tasmiya*.
- batin: interior, secret, esoteric.
- bay'at al-Ridhwan: the vow of allegiance given to Muhammad by 1,400 faithful at Hudaybiyya (Koran 14:18).
- bayt: house; the house par excellence is the House of God, the Ka'ba.
- Buraq: the mystical force the Prophet rode during his Night Journey (*mi'raj*).
- burda: woolen cloak. A famous example is the one the Prophet gave to Ka'b ibn Zuhayr for having composed and recited a poem for him. Passed on to the Abbasids, it is now in the pavilion of the Holy Mantle in the Topkapi Palace Museum, Istanbul. The word is also the name of a famous poem by al-Busiri in honor of Muhammad.

C

- caliph (*khalifah*): literally, successor; vicar, substitute, representative, lieutenant. Adam was the vicar of God on earth; he who governs, who is the vicar of God with temporary powers; also the "provincial father" of a Sufi confraternity. The first four caliphs that succeeded the Prophet Muhammad are known as the rightly guided caliphs.
- caravan (Persian: *karwan*): a company of travelers; a procession for the transport of goods on camels or mules (composed of as many as 2,500 animals, usually between 600 and 1,000 camels and 400 mules). The most important and the oldest caravan route was the Silk Road, controlled by the Turks, which was composed of a large network of caravansaries made of stone or brick. In Arabia

there was the Incense Road. With the advent of Islam the Cairo–Mecca caravans of pilgrims came to number as many as 30,000 to 40,000 camels, for a trip of forty days.

D

- dar al'Ilm: house of science, the name for the libraries and scientific institutes of the Islamic world around the tenth and eleventh centuries. Also *dar al-hikma*, house of wisdom; *dar al ulum*, house of the sciences.
- Dar al-salam: house of peace, a name once given to the entire Muslim world, more often called *dar al-Islam* in contrast to the non-Muslim territories, called the *dar al-harb*, the house of war.
- dhikr: remembrance. Cited many times in the Koran, it became the distinctive ritual of the Sufis, during which names of God and specific religious formulas are repeated in a singsong with or without the accompaniment of chants and music. Relatively similar to the *sema*.
- divorce: *see* talaq

F

- faqir: poor. Arabic term also used to indicate the Sufi (in Asia, *darwish*), meaning he who follows a mystical path (*tariqa*).
- fatiha: Opener; title of the first sura of the Koran with which all the prayers of the Muslim begin.
- fatwa: decision, sentence, legal response. The ruling on matters of Islamic religious law expressed by a *mufti*.
- fiqh: jurisprudence; Muslim canonical law; jurisdiction; science of the law.
- Friday: *see* jum'ah.
- futuwwa: "Youth and chivalry"; brotherhood or guild of artisans held to irreprehensible behavior. Also refers to an aspect of the Sufi confraternity.

G

- ghanima: spoils, the earnings from a raid, which for the early Arabs was a legitimate means of getting income. The Arabs had special rules for the division of spoils gotten during a war or raid.

H

- Hadith: story, speech, report, news, account, saying; the deeds or words of the Prophet or descriptions of the acts of the Prophet, as provided by the testimony of his companions or friends, that are supplementary to the Koran. The Hadith constitute "the Tradition," the *sunna*, which became a science of the tradition, one of the three principal branches of Islamic theology. The Hadith are arranged on a scale of forty-four values, from the most certain to the least probable.
- hajj: ritual pilgrimage to Mecca, Arafat, and Mina; one of the five obligations, or pillars

(*arkan*), of the Muslim. It is "conditional" since it depends on specific conditions of the pilgrim and the safety of the territory to be crossed.

• hal (plural *ahwal*): important term of Sufism indicating a spiritual state, a moment of extrasensory or mystical perception of a transitory nature; a level of permanent spiritual evolution is called *maqam*.

• halal: legal; that which is religiously legal. For example, in order to be halal (fit for consumption) meat must be butchered following a certain ritual, with a clean cut of the carotid artery while pronouncing the name of God, expulsion of all the blood, with the head of the animal turned toward Mecca.

• halqa: circle. Gathering of people assembled to form a circle; the gathering of students around their teacher; the gathering of Sufis around a master. A council of sages.

• hammam: Turkish bath, the typical, sometimes large-scale structure composed of at least three principal rooms, without windows. The basic rooms include the dressing room (*mushallah*) with services; the warm room to undress in the winter; cold room; hot room (*tahmim*); and rooms for massage.

• hanif (plural *hunafa*): believer in an original monotheistic religion, before Islam. The patriarch Abraham is the hanif par excellence.

• haram: illegal, forbidden, the category of actions, foods, and thoughts that the Muslim must not accept.

• harb: war. To be legal, both in the pre-Islamic world and in the Islamic, war must follow certain rules and legal conventions, both for its declaration and for its conduct.

• harem (Turkish form of the term *harim*): the area of a house to which access is forbidden to men, thus the apartments of the women that are off-limits to males who are not relatives or do not have permission.

• hegira: breaking with family ties; the "emigration" of the Prophet from Mecca to Medina in September 622; usually translated in the West as "flight." It is celebrated on the first day of the month of Rabi al-Awwal. Those who accompanied Muhammad on the emigration are called *muhajirun*. In response to unanimous agreement the date of the hegira was used by the first caliph, Abu Bakr, as the starting point for the years of Islam; in accordance with the Muslim lunar calendar the date was July 16, 611. To find the Gregorian year (G), beginning with an Islamic year (H) use this formula: H:33=X. H−X=Y. Y+622=G.

• hell: *see* jahannam

• hijab: veil, from the verb *hajaba*, subtract from the eyes, hide; separation. Head scarf that hides the hair, a costume of various populations, including those not Islamic (established by St. Paul for Christians: I Corinthians 11:6); it is imposed on women most of all by Arabian and Arabic-speaking fundamentalists but is not obligatory according to the Koran, and verse 24:31, the only reference to anything similar, takes it as a "mantle that covers the chest," and as such is explained by the Hadith

(Bukhari, LXV: 24:12). It is used in cities, but not among the Bedouin, peasants, and many laborers. Not recommended by the viceroy Egypt Isma (1873), it was opposed by Qasim Amin (1863–1912) and the theologian Muhammad Abduh.

• hijra: *see* hegira

• holidays: Laylat al-Qadr, the "Night of Destiny," 27 Ramadan; Id al-Fitr, celebration of breaking the fast, on the first day of the month of Sawwal; Mawlid al-Nabi, birthday of the Prophet, 12 First Rabi; Laylat al-Mir'aj, "Night of the Ascension," 27 Rajab; Id al-Adha, the "feast of the sacrifice," 10 Du al-Hijjah, an obligatory holiday, its celebrations usually last three days. There are three other optional holidays: the last Friday of Ramadan; Laylat al-Bara'ah (Shab i-Barat), 15 Shaban; and Ashura, 10 Muharram, a holiday particularly popular with Shiites. There is also the first of Muharram, the day of the hegira, the "emigration" of the Prophet from Mecca, the beginning of the Muslim year, and the entire month of Ramadan.

I

• ijma: the unanimous accord of the community (*umma*); the doctrine and unanimous opinion of recognized theologians in relation to a question or rule of religion. This is the third and perhaps most important base of Islamic religious law.

• ijtihad: *see* jihad

• ilhad: heresy, atheism; the attitude of the *mulhid* (deviationist, heretic, apostate). During the early period of Islam it also had a political connotation in terms of the rejection of constituted authority.

• ilm: science, knowledge, doctrine, learning.

• imam: the guide of common prayer; founder of a legal school; theologian that has acquired competence in matters of doctrine.

• iman: the faith, both in its practice and its contents. From the root *mn*: to confide, to recover; sincerity, faith.

• inshallah *(in sha Allah)*: if it pleases God; if God wishes.

• isha: nocturnal canonical prayer.

• ishrak: idolatry, polytheism; multiplicity, association.

• islah: reform, reformism.

• Islam: submission to the will of God. From the root *slm*, which has the sense of submission, hence the terms *salam*, peace; Muslim; *aslama*, embrace; Islam; *salima*, safe, irreprehensible.

• isma: infallibility (quality that no human being possesses); impeccability (absolute impeccability is the exclusive trait of the Prophet Muhammad).

• isnad: the chain of transmission ("who told whom") of a tradition (Hadith).

J

• jahannam: hell, Gehenna.

• jahiliyya: ignorance, paganism; the age of ignorance in which the Arabian peoples lived before Islam.

• jihad: effort, force. The Koran distinguishes a minor effort (*alijhad alasghar*), such as participating in a battle or defending oneself from an attack, from a greater effort, performed within oneself to overcome a negative inclination or selfishness. It cannot be properly translated as "holy war" despite its use with that meaning among certain extremist factions and so-called Islamic fundamentalists. "Holy" is *quds* and "war" is *harb*. *Ijtihad* (literally, to endeavor) refers to the effort made to arrive at a just decision.

• jizya: capitation tax that Islamic law applies to non-Muslim minorities living in Islamic territory, the *dhimma* that intend to follow their own religion and customs. The tax must be paid only by free, able-bodied, adult males.

• jum'ah: Friday, day of canonical common prayer at the moment when the sun leaves the zenith.

K

• kafir: unbeliever.

• kahin: among pre-Islamic Arabs, the person who performed the functions of augur, performer of sacrifices, fortune-teller, and prophet. At the beginning of his calling the Prophet was accused by the Meccans of wanting to be a *kahin*.

• khalifa: *see* caliph

• kharaj: obligatory charity; tax.

• Kharijites (withdrawers): members of the oldest heterodox Islamic sect. Promoters of a puritanical version of Islam, they caused many revolutions and much bloodshed between the seventh and eighth centuries.

• khatam al-Anbiya: Seal of the Prophecy, a designation of the Prophet Muhammad.

• kuttab: elementary school, an institution that came into being in the Islamic world early in the eighth century.

L

• Labbayka: "Here I am," exclaimed by a pilgrim on arrival in Mecca.

• Laylat al-Qadar: the "Night of Destiny," traditionally celebrated on 27 Ramadan, in memory of the night in the year 610 in which the revelation of the Koran began.

M

• madrasa: scholastic institution for the teaching of Islamic sciences; school of superior studies; university faculty. The word also refers to the architectural structure that hosts the school, which is usually somewhat similar to a mosque, the origins of which are in the *vihara* of central Asia beginning in the seventh and eighth centuries.

• manara: *see* minaret

• masha Allah (*masciallah*): what God wants. Koranic expression much used by people in a superstitious sense to ward off evil.

• masjid: *see* mosque

• mihrab: the large niche located in the wall facing the Ka'ba in a mosque, oratory, or any place of prayer: it indicates the direction to be taken in prayer (*qibla*). Made in a great variety of materials (marble, carved wood, ceramic, and so on), it is the most important element in the mosque from the artistic point of view.

• minaret (from *manar*, lighthouse). Nonessential element rising over the mosque from which the muezzin calls the faithful to prayer (*adhan*). In the opinion of certain scholars, the origins of the minaret lead back to the sepulchral towers of Palmyra, to ancient Egyptian obelisks, and to the *massebah* (commemorative funerary stela used by the peoples called Semitic); there are also those who trace the minaret back to Christian bell towers, but this seems less likely, since minarets appeared first. There are basically three main types of minarets: with square base (North Africa), organ pipe (central Asia), and needle (Turkey).

• milla: religion, religious doctrine, spiritual community.

• minbar: tribune or pulpit that flanks the mihrab to the right of the believer. It is used for Friday prayers (*khutba*).

• mi'raj: stairs, ascension. The prophetic Night Journey of Muhammad from Medina to Jerusalem and from the rock of the Temple Mount of Jerusalem to the heavens; traditionally celebrated on the 27th day of the month of Rajab.

• mithaq: pact, alliance.

• mosque (*masjid*): literally, the place of prostration; the principal site of worship in Islam, the place where the community gathers, most of all Friday when the sun reaches the zenith. It can also serve the functions of elementary school, court, or mausoleum. The classical structure includes a large niche (*mihrab*) on the wall facing the Ka'ba that indicates the direction to take in prayer (*qibla*); a pulpit (*minbar*); and usually also a minaret.

• mufti: jurist; he that emits the *fatwa*.

• muhajir: exile, emigrant. The *Muhajirun* were those Muslims that followed the Prophet in his emigration from Mecca to Medina; they then formed the base for Muhammad's political power.

• mu'min: believer, monotheist that believes in God, no matter to which religion he belongs.

• munafiq: hypocrite; a person whose behavior is strongly condemned by the Koran (one of the four attributes of the fanatic: hypocrisy, presumption, ignorance, paranoia).

• muqarnas: decorative form typical of Islamic architecture. The term is derived from the Greek *koronis*. It is used as a connection between a horizontal plane and one vertical, similar to the vault common to Romanesque-Gothic architecture. *Muqarnas* are decorated in three-dimensional tiers, whether of stone or wood, brick or ceramic. They are also used to decorate capitals, the intradoses of arches, or the interior or exterior surfaces of domes.

• muslih: reformer, rectifier, restorer.

• muslimun: the Muslims. Two distinct groups of Muslim communities can be found in Europe, those "antique," dating to as early as the fourteenth century, the results of Mongolian and Turkish invasions (Greece, Bulgaria, Romania, Albania, and other Balkan countries; Hungary, Poland, Finland), and those "recent," the result of the immigration to the industrialized countries of Europe of Muslims from the rest of the world.

P
• pilgrimage: *see* hajj

Q
• qibla: *see* masjid

• Quraysh: one of the most powerful tribes of Mecca, founded by the leader Fihr, of the Kinana tribe. The name is the diminutive of *qirsh*, meaning "shark." The sixth descendant of Fihr, Qusayy, conquered the sanctuary of Mecca and divided the city among the various branches of his tribe, from one of which came the Prophet.

R
• Ramadan: ninth month of the Muslim calendar; sacred because it was in that month that the Koran began "descending" on Muhammad. The month is dedicated to fasting in accordance with precise rules.

S
• salam: health, peace; salaam. The typical greeting that the Muslim exchanges with other Muslims; *al-Salam alaykum (wa ramat allah wa barakatu)*, to which the response is *wa alaykum salam*.

• salat: ordinary ritual or canonical prayer, performed five times a day: at dawn (*fajr*), when the sun leaves the zenith (*zuhr*), the end of afternoon (*asr*), after sunset (*maghrib*), and at the onset of night (*isha*).

• sawm: fast; the fast prescribed by Islamic law.

• sema (sama): collective spiritual ritual typical of the Sufis, accompanied by singing and music. It is relatively similar to the *dhikr*.

• Shahada: declaration of faith, attestation to the singleness of God and the mission of the Prophet, using the formula *la ilaha illa Allah, Muhammad rasul Allah:* "There is no god but God, and Muhammad is the messenger of God."

• Shari'a: religious law; traditional laws.

• shaykh: *see* sheikh

• sheikh (shaykh), also sheik: the elder, the leader, the master; the spiritual guide, the founder of a Sufi confraternity.

• Shia: the sect, the sect of the followers of Ali, as opposed to the Sunni.

• Sira: conduct, itinerary; the discipline or science that studies the circumstances of the life of the Prophet and his behavior.

• Sufism (Tasawwuf): the way, the mystical initiation, divided in orders or confraternities (*turuq*, singular *tariqa*). Its esoteric character, based on the profound understanding of the Koran; its respect for all faiths; its love of knowledge, higher learning, the arts, and their values make it one of the outstanding expressions of Islam.

• Sunna: rules of life; the tradition of Islam based on the acts and words of the Prophet as a complement and explication of the Koran.

• sura: division, level, fence. Each of the 114 divisions of the Koran is a sura, erroneously called "chapter" by some authors.

T
• talaq: divorce. Name of the sixty-fifth sura of the Koran.

• tanasukh: metempsychosis, reincarnation. Some Sufi confraternities interpret three verses of the Koran (in particular 3:27 and 40:11) to support this hypothesis.

• Tasawwuf: *see* Sufism

• tawhid: singleness, the uniqueness of God; the unity and transcendence of God, the heart of Islamic faith.

U
• umma: community. The traditional community of the Muslims.

• ummi: illiterate, unlearned; attributed to the Prophet with the meaning of not having knowledge of the sacred Jewish and Christian texts.

• umra: the small or ordinary pilgrimage to visit Mecca, which can be made at any time of the year except during the period of the great pilgrimage.

W
• wudu: ablution. The ritual ablution that must precede prayers when the person about to pray is not in a state of purity. There are greater and lesser ablutions involving the washing of hands, mouth, nostrils, face, forearms, hands, hair, ears, and feet. In the absence of water there is the dry ablution (*tayammum*), which involves the use of sand or earth while resting the hands on clean surfaces.

Y
• yawm al-Dyn: the day of judgment.

Z
• zakat: charity; one of the five obligations of the Muslim.

Bibliography

Ahmed, Akbar S. *Living Islam: From Samarkand to Stornoway*. London: BBC Books, 1993.

Bennett, Clinton. *In Search of Muhammad*. London and New York: Cassell, 1998.

Crone, Patricia. *Meccan Trade and the Rise of Islam*. Princeton: Princeton University Press, 1987.

Esposito, John L., ed. *The Oxford History of Islam*. Oxford, New York: Oxford University Press, 1999.

Glassé, Cyril. *Concise Encyclopedia of Islam*. London: Stacey International, 1989.

Hiro, Dilip. *Islamic Fundamentalism*. London: Paladin, 1988.

Lewis, Bernard. *The Arabs in History*. 5th ed. London: Hutchinson University Library, 1970.

------. *The Crisis of Islam: Holy War and Unholy Terror*. New York: Modern Library, 2003.

------. *What Went Wrong? Western Impact and Middle Eastern Response*. Oxford, New York: Oxford University Press, 2002.

Lewis, Bernard, ed. and trans. *Islam, from the Prophet Muhammad to the Capture of Constantinople*. New York: Harper & Row, 1974.

McAuliffe, Jane Dammen, ed. *Encyclopedia of the Quar'an*. Leiden: Brill, 2001.

Nasr, Seyyed Hossein. *Islamic Life and Thought*. London: Allen and Unwin, 1981.

------. *A Young Muslim's Guide to the Modern World*. Chicago: Kazi Publications, 1994.

Riddell, Peter G. and Peter Cotterell. *Islam in Context: Past, Present, and Future*. Grand Rapids: Baker Academic, 2003.

Rippin, Andrew. *Muslims: Their Religious Beliefs and Practices*. 2nd ed. London: Routledge, 2001.

Robinson, Francis, ed. *Cambridge Illustrated History of the Islamic World*. Cambridge: Cambridge University Press, 1996.

Rodinson, Maxime. *Mohammed*. Harmondsworth: Penguin, 1971.

Rodwell, J. M., trans. *The Koran*. London: Everyman, 1909.

Ruthven, Malise. *Islam in the World*. 2nd ed. London: Penguin, 2000.

Watt, W. Montgomery. *Early Islam*. Edinburgh: Edinburgh University Press, 1990.

------. *The Majesty That Was Islam*. London: Sidgwick and Jackson, 1974.